THE BEGINNER'S GUIDE TO

How to
BUILD, MAINTAIN,
and EXPERIENCE
a MUSIC
COLLECTION
in ANALOG

Vinyl

JENNA MI

A adamsmedia
Avon, Massachusetts

Published by
Adams Media, a division of F+W Media, Inc.
57 Littlefield Street, Avon, MA 02322. U.S.A.
www.adamsmedia.com

ISBN 10: 1-4405-9896-7
ISBN 13: 978-1-4405-9896-8
eISBN 10: 1-4405-9897-5
eISBN 13: 978-1-4405-9897-5

Printed in the United States of America.

10 9 8 7 6 5 4 3 2 1

Library of Congress Cataloging-in-Publication Data

Miles, Jenna.
The beginner's guide to vinyl / Jenna Miles.
Avon, Massachusetts: Adams Media, 2017.
Includes index.
LCCN 2016032064 (print) | LCCN 2016033598 (ebook) | ISBN 9781440598968 (pb) | ISBN 1440598967 (pb) | ISBN 9781440598975 (ebook) | ISBN 1440598975 (ebook)
LCSH: Sound recordings--Collectors and collecting. | Phonograph. | Sound recordings--History.
LCC ML1055 .M45 2016 (print) | LCC ML1055 (ebook) | DDC 780.26/6--dc23
LC record available at https://lccn.loc.gov/2016032064

Readers are urged to take all appropriate precautions before undertaking any how-to task. Always read and follow instructions and safety warnings for all tools and materials, and call in a professional if the task stretches your abilities too far. Although every effort has been made to provide the best possible information in this book, neither the publisher nor the author is responsible for accidents, injuries, or damage incurred as a result of tasks undertaken by readers. This book is not a substitute for professional services.

This publication is designed to provide accurate and authoritative information with regard to the subject matter covered. It is sold with the understanding that the publisher is not engaged in rendering legal, accounting, or other professional advice. If legal advice or other expert assistance is required, the services of a competent professional person should be sought.
—From a *Declaration of Principles* jointly adopted by a Committee of the American Bar Association and a Committee of Publishers and Associations

Many of the designations used by manufacturers and sellers to distinguish their products are claimed as trademarks. Where those designations appear in this book and F+W Media, Inc. was aware of a trademark claim, the designations have been printed with initial capital letters.

Cover design by Colleen Cunningham.
Cover and interior images © kaspri/123RF; iStockphoto/RG-vc.
Interior illustrations by Eric Andrews.
Insert photographs by Giulio Bevacqua.

This book is available at quantity discounts for bulk purchases.
For information, please call 1-800-289-0963.

Contents ‍N

Introduction... 7

1 The History of Vinyl: How a Record Is Made 9

PHONAUTOGRAPH.. 10
PHONOGRAPH.. 10
GRAPHOPHONE... 11
GRAMOPHONE.. 12
COMMERCIALIZATION OF RECORDS—
 THE RECORD LABELS 12
THE FIRST RECORD LABELS (1880S–1930)..................... 14
RPMS—RECORDING TIME AND SPACE......................... 20
VINYL RECORD MATERIALS 25
UNUSUAL, OBSCURE, AND CREATIVE RECORDS............. 31

2 How Records Are Made 35

AN OVERVIEW 36
RECORD THE SOUND 36
SOUND PLAYBACK 38
CREATING THE LACQUER.. 40
PLATING 42
TEST PRESSINGS 43
PRESSING A RECORD.. 44
VINYL RECORD JACKETS AND ARTWORK 47

3 Turntables 101 51

ANATOMY OF A TURNTABLE 52
OTHER TURNTABLE TERMINOLOGY 60
THE PREAMP 63
RECEIVER 65
SPEAKERS 66

4 Purchasing a Turntable.. 69

WHAT ARE YOUR NEEDS?...................................... 70
TURNTABLE SETUP COMPONENTS............................. 71
BUYING A USED OR VINTAGE TURNTABLE..................... 71
PURCHASING A NEW TURNTABLE 81
SETTING UP YOUR TURNTABLE................................ 101
A FEW DON'TS FOR CARING FOR YOUR TURNTABLE ... 105
CLEANING THE STYLUS... 107
REPLACING YOUR CARTRIDGE/STYLUS 108

5 Vinyl Collectors' Terminology 111

THE PLURAL OF VINYL IS NOT VINYLS . . . OR IS IT?.... 112
AUDIOPHILE... 112
REMASTERED 114
MASTERED FROM THE ORIGINAL SOURCE 114
DIRECT METAL MASTERING (DMM) 115
MATRIX AREA/DEAD WAX... 115
RECORD WEIGHT... 116
ETCHING.. 116
JACKET TYPES.. 116
2LP, 3LP, 4LP QUAD LP, DOUBLE LP, AND MORE!.......... 117
RECORD SLEEVES 118
OLD VERSUS NEW.. 119

6 Purchasing Used Records..................................... 121

EXAMINING AND INSPECTING USED RECORDS 122
GRADING USED RECORDS.. 126
WHERE TO BUY USED VINYL 128
PURCHASING USED VINYL ONLINE 132

7 Purchasing New Vinyl 135

NEW VINYL–SPECIFIC CONSIDERATIONS 136
WHERE TO BUY NEW VINYL... 137
BOOTLEG RECORDS 145

8 Storing Records 147

HOW TO PROPERLY HANDLE A RECORD...................... 148
PROPER METHODS FOR STORING YOUR COLLECTION. 150
RECORD SLEEVES 152
RECORD STORAGE IDEAS 156
INSURING YOUR RECORD COLLECTION 162

9 Cleaning and Repairing Records........................... 167

ALWAYS START WITH A CLEAN RECORD...................... 168
WET CLEANING 169
DRY CLEANING... 176
RECORD-CLEANING METHODS TO AVOID................... 178
HOW TO FIX A WARPED RECORD................................. 180
FIXING SCRATCHES ON RECORDS 180

10 More Advanced Collecting 183

YOU'LL FIND SO MANY RECORDS TO CHOOSE FROM! 184
DIFFERENT PRESSINGS OF THE SAME ALBUM 185
ORIGINAL AND FIRST PRESSINGS 191
VINYL REISSUES 193
VINYL REISSUES FROM RECORD LABELS 194
PROMOTIONAL RECORDS 206
TEST PRESSINGS 208
VALUABLE RECORDS 209
RECORD STORE DAY 209

11 Vinyl and the Internet 213

EXACTLY HOW DID THE INTERNET FUEL THE VINYL
  REVIVAL? 214
ONLINE COMMUNITIES 216
VINYL MEDIA AND NEWS ONLINE 225
FUN SITES TO VISIT 228
RESOURCEFUL WEBSITES 229
PHONE AND TABLET APPS 237
YOUTUBE 239

Glossary 241

Top Indie Record Stores 249

Index 253

Introduction

Vinyl records are back—in a big way. More and more music lovers are forgoing digital files and turning back to vinyl for its pure sound, more complete listening experience, and the fun of collecting. Whether your musical tastes are jazz, rock, country, classical, or show tunes, you can find vinyl records from your favorite artists.

If you're brand-new to vinyl, this book will walk you through all the basics—how records are made, how to purchase a record player (which is actually called a "turntable"), and how to take care of both the machine and your vinyl records. If you're a more advanced audiophile, you'll find plenty of information about machinery beyond the entry-level options, along with intriguing tidbits and stories about artists and the industry that you've never heard before.

Once you've learned about the equipment, you can delve into building or expanding your vinyl collection. You might choose to search online for a particular album you just *have* to have. Or you might prefer browsing at your local independent record store to see what cool surprises await you. Either way, I'll make sure that you become a master at finding used records that are in good shape and are a great value.

My venture into the world of vinyl began accidently in 2006. My spouse and I were running an online radio station, PunkRadioCast, which had built a dedicated listening audience, one of the largest in online radio at its time, but not so successful in monetizing since Internet radio was still in its infancy. Due to the recession's impact on the music business, we had to make a change immediately. To keep our record label advertisers and friends on track, we offered them free advertising in exchange for "dead stock" they had laying around their warehouses—which often happened to be vinyl. We created a little marketplace within PunkRadioCast called ShopRadioCast, in which we sold this product to our large listening audience. Little did we realize that these small trades would grow into what is now known as SRCVinyl, a leading independent online retailer of vinyl and one of the larger vinyl-only reissue labels.

During the early years of SRCVinyl, we discovered a website, Vinyl Collective (www.vinylcollective.com), a large community of vinyl collectors that we acquired in early 2011. Prior to the vinyl boom, I would spend countless hours searching through various record labels' and distributors' inventories, finding tons of hidden gems that vinyl collectors were on the hunt for. As the market grew and these old records became more and more scarce and our vinyl-buying audience grew, we decided to look into working with the record labels to release titles on vinyl. To date, we have released just under 100 albums and have overseen the production of hundreds of thousands of records on vinyl. In 2015, we opened up a retail store in Niagara Falls, Canada, with a retail shop opening up in Toronto shortly after. I spend a lot of my day buying vinyl to stock our online and brick-and-mortar stores, researching titles to release next, listening to test pressings for upcoming projects, reviewing and brainstorming artwork for our releases, and maintaining the Vinyl Collective website. Over the last ten years, I have spent just about every day (I do not take many weekends off) living and breathing vinyl. Once you get used to hearing the warm, rich sounds of vinyl, you might never go back to your digital music player. Let's get started!

CHAPTER 1

The History of Vinyl: How a Record Is Made

*V*inyl record production began in the middle of the nineteenth century, during the second Industrial Revolution, an era that saw many of history's notable inventors formulate and refine technologies, significantly altering history. By the late nineteenth century, there were three patented records and accompanying turntables—the phonograph, Graphophone, and gramophone. These three terms are often applied interchangeably when referring to vinyl records, under the assumption they convey the same meaning. However, they were, in fact, three distinct devices. Each one has significantly contributed to the development of not only how vinyl is made today but the creation of the music industry and the birth of the record label.

Phonautograph

Although it was never developed into an actual sound play-back device, the phonautograph is the earliest known mechanism that had the ability to record sound, paving the path to the possibility of the record player. It was invented and patented by Édouard-Léon Scott de Martinville in 1857 as an apparatus to graphically record sound with a stylus. The device used a horn to collect sound and was attached to a diaphragm that vibrated a strong bristle. The bristle inscribed an image on a cylinder that was coated in black ink. The intent was to visually record audio for the purpose of studying sound properties, and it did not offer any audio playback. (Prior to the 1870s, no one knew how to play back sound.)

Phonograph

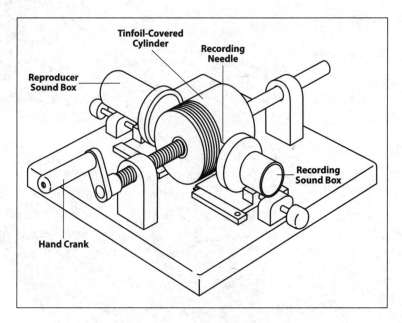

In 1876, Alexander Graham Bell obtained the first patent for the telephone, after he and other inventors had worked on various iterations for decades. During this time, Thomas Edison set out to create an accompanying telephone recorder. Instead, he invented the "phonograph," a contraption that was patented in 1877. It had the ability to both record and play back sound. The phonograph operated an electromagnet to vibrate a steel stylus, which recorded the sound to tinfoil that was wrapped around a grooved metal cylinder as it rotated. Once recorded, the sound could be played back immediately. Throughout 1878, Edison created 500 tinfoil phonographs for the purpose of demonstration. Following this, Edison pursued other projects and played no further role in the development of the phonograph and phonograph records until approximately a decade later.

Graphophone

The phonograph's first opponent, the Graphophone, was invented by Alexander Graham Bell's Volta Laboratory in Washington, D.C. Under the supervision of Charles Sumner Tainter and Chichester Bell (Alexander Graham Bell's cousin), it took Volta Laboratory a total of five years to invent the Graphophone. The major difference from the phonograph was the use of wax instead of tinfoil, which resulted in better sound quality, recording time capabilities, and durability. The Graphophone utilized a lateral recording technique, whereas Edison's phonograph used vertically cut grooves. With these enhancements, Bell's Graphophone qualified for its own patent, granted in 1880.

12 Gramophone

In 1889, Emile Berliner introduced and patented a version of the record player that was intended for commercial use that he named the gramophone. Instead of using a cylinder as a medium to hold the recorded audio, the gramophone contained a zinc disc coated with wax. After the recording was carved into the wax, the disc would at this point be dipped into an acid solution. This solution would eat away at the zinc beneath and create an etched groove on the surface. The zinc disc was now the stamper that was employed to manufacture the end product. Improvements to the gramophone discs kicked off the ability to easily mass-produce records.

HOW DO RECORDS PLAY MUSIC?
Here's how a modern record plays sound: When a stylus (needle on a turntable) hits the groove of a record, it glides through various peaks and valleys that have been sculpted into the record groove, creating vibrations. These vibrations are converted into electrical signals, which are then outputted into a speaker.

Commercialization of Records—The Record Labels

In 1889, "phonograph parlors" began to open up, marking the debut of phonographs to the mass market. The first phonograph parlor opened in San Francisco in May 1889. Almost all American cities had at least one by the mid-1890s. These parlors allowed customers to sit at a desk and speak through a tube to request a recorded title. The title would then play through a cylinder phonograph from a room located below, allowing customers to listen to it through two ear horns at their private desk.

At the time, the mass production of records was still in its infancy and was genuinely primitive. One of the first recording methods had live performers record their tracks onto a phonograph, filling up to ten tubes leading to blank cylinders within other phonographs. Even with this method the artist was required to rerecord a song multiple times.

Until the early 1900s, both cylinder and disc recordings were available. In terms of audio fidelity, gramophone discs were not superior to cylinder records. The disc method, on the other hand, did provide further manufacturing advantages, since discs could be efficiently stamped allowing them to be easily mass-produced.

WHAT IS FIDELITY?
When referring to audio, fidelity indicates how accurately a copy of an album sounds in comparison to the master version. When an album has been mastered with the highest quality, it is often referred to as a high fidelity, or "hi-fi," referencing the high-quality reproduction. Albums reproduced with audio flaws such as distortion, static, and other background noise are referred to as low fidelity, or "lo-fi." Additionally, the electronic equipment used to play an album, such as turntable and speakers, can also be "hi-fi" or "lo-fi" quality and in turn affect the output of the audio.

Emile Berliner's disc records, the first offered to the public, were initially 5 inches in diameter and recorded on one side only. In 1895, Berliner offered 7-inch records, and by 1901 the gramophone was available in 10-inch records. The Berliner discs were the ancestor of what we know today as the 78-, 45-, and 33⅓-rpm analog records.

The First Record Labels (1880s–1930)

Once the devices were invented, businesses sprang up around it to manufacturer music and commercial products.

Edison's Phonograph

Although Edison initially stopped working on his phonograph after patenting it, he did return to work on the phonograph and a phonograph cylinder around 1887. By 1888, he launched Edison Records. In this launch, Edison Records unveiled what they called the "Perfected Phonograph," a wax cylinder approximately 4¼ inches long and 2¼ inches in diameter. This Edison cylinder record played at a speed of 120 rpm and could hold approximately 3 minutes of recording. By the turn of the century, the Edison cylinder speed was increased to 160 rpm. This improved the sound quality, but decreased the playback length to about 2 minutes and 15 seconds.

Early on, blank records were an integral part of Edison's business. The majority of phonographs included an attachment for users to generate their own recording, which was commonly for dictation purposes. Entertainment cylinders and phonographs were introduced in 1889, but were costly and hazardous due to their electric motor and therefore were primarily only accessed in public facilities, such as arcades and salons.

Home entertainment phonographs and cylinders were introduced in the mid-1890s with the creation of a more cost-effective phonograph. Edison's laboratory was also credited for its ability to mass-produce prerecorded phonographs. In

1902, Edison's company (named National Phonograph Company at that time) introduced the Edison Gold Moulded Records. These were cylinders made from a hard black wax, as opposed to the brown wax previously used that was soft and quickly deteriorated. The new, harder black wax cylinders could be played hundreds of times before wearing out. Edison developed a process that utilized a mold made from a master cylinder, allowing them to produce several hundred cylinders from a single mold. These new cylinders were named Gold Moulded Records because of a gold vapor given off by gold electrodes used during the production process.

EDISON WAS HARD OF HEARING

Although Thomas Edison was the inventor of the phonograph and one of the early leaders in developing the music industry, he was actually hard of hearing.

In 1908, Edison launched a state-of-the-art line of cylinder —the Amberol. These cylinders could play up to 4 minutes of music. This was achieved by creating smaller grooves that were closer together. By 1912, Edison introduced Blue Amberol Records, a cylinder record made from a type of plastic that was tinted a trademarked blue. These new and improved Amberols played for as long as 4 minutes and 45 seconds at a speed of 160 rpm. The Amberol records could be played back over 3,000 times.

In 1912, the Edison company succumbed to the popularity of the disc and once and for all made the switch to a 10-inch disc record, titled Edison Diamond Disc. In comparison to the other disc records available, Edison's 10-inch disc was significantly thicker—¼ inch—to avoid warping. Edison continued to record sound vertically in the groove at 150 grooves per inch, which is referred to as "hill-and-dale" recording. The majority of other companies were cutting their records laterally at 100 grooves per inch. This gave Edison's disc records a longer playing time than his competitors, now up to 5 minutes.

Edison's brand-new records were titled Diamond Disc because the matching phonograph player included a semi-permanent diamond stylus as opposed to the metal styluses previously applied. The combination of these upgraded discs and diamond stylus players produced a high-quality audio product that was superior to its competitors. Edison's discs and players were costlier and were not adaptable with other players on the market due to their vertically cut grooves.

FIRST 12-INCH RECORDING

To coincide with RCA Victor's launch of the "LP," or long-play album, the first record that could hold up to 15 minutes per side, they pressed Beethoven's Fifth Symphony, which was performed by the Philadelphia Orchestra.

The Edison discs saw great success up until the 1920s, with a sales peak occurring in the year of 1920. Although Diamond Discs were higher fidelity and longer playing than the competitors, the Edison catalog was limited to old-fashioned musical performers and was out of touch with the jazz record–buying public throughout this time.

In 1926, Edison Records attempted a revival with the introduction of the long-playing record. Edison achieved a playing time of 24 minutes on 10-inch discs and 40 minutes on 12-inch discs. Due to problems with skipping and low volume, however, only fourteen Edison Long Play discs were created before they were discontinued.

When electric recording began in 1927, the Edison company was the last to adapt to this method. Edison still made both disc and cylinder records commercially accessible until he discontinued cylinder manufacturing in the fall of 1929. Sales continued to drop and Edison Records (coincidentally) closed their doors just one day before the 1929 stock market crash. After the closure of Edison Records, Henry Ford bought an abundance of the recordings and metal masters and added them to the Henry Ford Museum. In 2001, the Henry Ford Museum donated its metal molds to the Edison

EDISON RECORDS TODAY

During the 1990s, Shawn Borri of Borri Audio Laboratories purchased the assets of the North American Phonograph Company. Since then, Borri Audio Laboratories has manufactured more than 10,000 new blank and custom-recorded cylinder records. Borri Audio Laboratories also offers repair and restoration of recorded cylinders, and parts and equipment for Edison collectors.

National Historic Site in New Jersey. The Edison National Historic Site currently preserves approximately 11,000 cylinder phonograph records, 28,000 disc phonograph records, and 9,800 disc metal molds.

Recently, the Edison National Historic Site recorded select phonographs digitally and made them accessible through their website in MP3 format. The content of these recordings varies from popular music of that era to speeches, soundtracks, educational lessons, and more. Digitized recordings of Edison's records can be streamed from the Edison National Historic Site archive at www.nps.gov/edis/learn/photosmultimedia/the-recording-archives.htm and from the audio curator at Edison National Historic Site at http://wfmu.org/playlists/te.

American Graphophone Company/ Columbia Records (Bell)

Following the announcement of Volta Laboratory's Graphophone invention, the Volta Graphophone Company was incorporated on February 3, 1886, to bring the Graphophone into the market. The Volta Graphophone Company merged with an organization led by businessmen from Philadelphia and was called the American Graphophone Company, which eventually became Columbia Records.

The initial launch of Columbia was in 1889 as the Columbia Phonograph Company. In its infancy, Columbia licensed and sold the Graphophone from Bell and Tainter as well as Edison's phonograph within the Washington, D.C., area. Columbia's business relationship with Edison was terminated in 1894 when Edison ceased providing them with blank cylinders. Edison's recipe was a well-kept secret, and Columbia couldn't easily replicate cylinders. The materials Edison applied to mold his phonographs were not labeled, and attempts by Columbia to steal secrets from Edison employees were not successful. Columbia was left frantically trying to find a way to produce records in-house.

In 1893, the president of Columbia Phonograph acquired control of the American Graphophone Company, with the companies consolidating around 1895. Columbia began operations in Canada in 1904 with offices in Toronto, Hamilton, Montreal, and Brantford. By 1906, Columbia had changed its name to the Columbia Graphophone Company. Throughout the entire twentieth century, Columbia Records continued as a leading company within the music industry and still exists as a record label today.

Victor Talking Machine Company (Emile Berliner)

Emile Berliner's gramophones began as discs; they looked similar to the records we recognize today. The gramophone was initially released only within the European market and was introduced commercially in the United States in 1894 under the company name Berliner Gramophone.

One challenge Berliner faced was that the sound quality of the disc gramophone was inferior to the cylinder records of the time. Berliner's manufacturing associate, Eldridge R. Johnson, was granted patents for his improvements on the gramophone's sound quality. In 1901, Berliner and Eldridge formed the Victor Talking Machine Company to combine their patents. Shortly after this merger, Berliner moved to Canada to oversee production at what is now known as the RCA Victor factory, where gramophones were manufactured. Today the RCA Victor factory still exists in Montreal, Canada, with a studio alongside a museum dedicated to Berliner.

Johnson remained in New Jersey as president of Victor Talking Machine operations.

Victor is frequently recognized by their well-known trade-marked logo, which consists of a fox terrier named Nipper listening to a gramophone. Over the years, Victor developed into one of the largest record and phonograph manufacturers. Victor's success was short-lived, however, as by the late 1920s, radio was adversely impacting the sales of phonographs. Johnson sold Victor Talking Machine to RCA in 1927.

Modern Evolution of Vinyl Records (1930s–Present)

Since the 1930s, the vinyl record industry has seen distinctive highs and lows, with speculation of possible extinction occurring several times. Undeterred by these rumors, the industry has seen consistent technological improvements in recording speed, materials, and the manufacturing process and procedures.

Understanding all these aspects of a record is fundamental for a collector, as there are many variations of records out there, especially when buying used records. As record time and speed evolved, consumers were presented with different speed options that required turntables with the ability to play these speeds. Records were not always made out of the same material, so care for one album might be slightly different than another. Records manufactured through different eras may sound significantly different to a newly re-pressed reissue. The following sections detail the different speeds and materials you might find when you purchase new or used records.

RPMs—Recording Time and Space

The speed at which a record spins is measured in rpm (revolutions per minute). Playing time of a record is dependent on the speeds a turntable is able to play and the groove spacing on the disc. The first phonographs were only able to play as little as 2 minutes of recording per side. In the process of attempting to lengthen the amount of recording time a record held, inventors discovered changing the rpm of a record allowed for longer recordings. Understanding rpm is important because even modern turntables and records are available in different speeds.

RPM DOESN'T EQUAL RECORD SIZE
Be aware, although most people associate the rpm of a record with an actual record size, diverse record sizes are available in different rpms. For example: 7-inch records are repeatedly referred to as 45s, even though you can get a 7-inch record at 33⅓ rpm.

Early Speeds

The first recordings were produced at varying speeds ranging from 60 rpm to 160 rpm. During the 1800s, Emile Berliner's early 7-inch disc records were pressed at a speed of 70 rpm, whereas Edison's cylinders played at 120–125 rpm. By the 1900s, Edison's cylinder played at 160 rpm.

78 RPM

By 1925, cylinder records began to phase out and shellac disc records (at 78 rpm) were becoming the standard. The 78-rpm speed was the standard speed until about 1931. During the 78-rpm era, both 10-inch records that had a playing time of 3 minutes and 12-inch records that had a 3½-minute playing time were common. By virtue of the popularity of 10-inch discs during the 78-rpm era, 10-inch discs today are regularly referred to as 78s. By 1924, the 12-inch shellacked 78-rpm record had a 4- to 5-minute playing time.

Columbia's 33⅓ RPM (LPs)

The first 33⅓-rpm "long playing" record initially entered the market in 1931. RCA Victor launched these revolutionary phonographs that spun at 33⅓ rpm. They were pressed on a 30-cm (11.81 inches) disc and had a playing time of 22 minutes. This record was made out of a flexible plastic disc and could play about 10 minutes per side. They achieved this by using shallower grooves placed closer together than found on 78-rpm records. Despite this revolutionary creation, the long-playing disc was initially a commercial failure, mainly because of timing. The Great Depression brought about financial hardships, and most consumers couldn't afford luxuries like records.

AN EIGHTEEN-HOUR ALBUM?
Sometime during the late 1890s, composer Erik Satie wrote "Vexations," a musical composition that was intended to be performed 840 times, lasting more than 18 hours. Vinyl versions with a pianist performing this piece do exist; however, the piece is only performed thirty-five times, totaling just over 50 minutes— meaning you must spin this record twenty-four times to hear the full composition.

On June 18, 1948, the Columbia Record Company hosted a suspenseful press conference in New York to dazzle everyone with the 33⅓-rpm "microgroove" record, which was the first album with the ability to play 20 minutes per side, as opposed to the previous standard of 5 minutes a side. The first microgroove LP released by Columbia was catalog number Columbia ML 4001, *Mendelssohn: Concerto in E Minor for Violin and Orchestra, Op. 64* (with soloist Nathan Milstein and Bruno Walter conducting the Philharmonic-Symphony

Orchestra of New York). The Library of Congress, which cur- rently holds the Columbia Records Paperwork Collection, shows the label order for this release, ML 4001, was written on March 1, 1948, indicating that Columbia began production on the first LPs at least three months prior to its announcement.

Shortly after Columbia's announcement, RCA Victor began releasing LPs in 1950, with other major American labels following suit. In the United Kingdom, Decca Records was the first to release LPs. Since the 1950s, the 33⅓-rpm, 12-inch disc is what is commonly released for full-length albums.

RCA Victor's 45 RPM and the EP

To rival Columbia's microgroove LP, RCA Victor introduced the extended-play (EP) album, which is a 45-rpm record that contains more music than a single but not enough for a full-length album (LP). While Columbia's LP boasted up to 22 minutes of music per side, RCA distributed tracks off an album across multiple 45s that could be stacked on a tall spindle up to about 6 inches high. This spindle and stacking mechanism was exclusive to the RCA-manufactured turntables. Once a side of the 45-rpm record finished playing, the turntable's tone arm (see Chapter 3 for a turntable diagram) moved away and the next record would drop from the spindle. The tone arm then swung back into place and the music would continue playing. Although each of the 45s was shorter in length than a full LP, the RCA player could theoretically play music continuously for a full hour from the stacked spindle.

RCA's 45-rpm EPs also had a larger center hole, which measured 1½ inches in diameter. As a result of the 45s being dropped from the spindle onto the player, the turntable was required to rapidly spin from a dead stop to 45 rpm. If they had used a small center hole, the speed would cause the record to wobble while it spun. To make 45s playable on other turntables, a 45 adapter, a tiny plastic insert that is placed in the middle of a larger-holed 45 so that it could be played on LP or 78 turntables, was introduced. Even though RCA eventually adapted to the 33⅓ LP during the 1950s, the 45-rpm speed has since been the standard speed for the single 7-inch record.

16⅔ RPM—Turntable Car Stereos

Ever since the mid-1950s, the common home record player typically had three to four speeds to accommodate the commonly found record speeds—78, 45, 33⅓, and 16⅔ rpm. Most people who had turntables with this fourth speed likely used the 16⅔ rpm to slow down their LPs and 45s (just for fun), and probably didn't even know where this fourth speed originated. Although rare, 16⅔-rpm records do exist. This speed is exactly half the speed of the commonly available 33⅓-rpm LPs. In order to achieve this speed, an extremely small groove dubbed the "ultra microgroove" was cut. These 16⅔-rpm records were released in various sizes for several decades; it first appeared in the 1930s, was most popular during the 1950s, and had essentially disappeared by the 1970s.

RECORDING TIMES
Records can hold more speech than music. Why? The amount and volume of audio affects the size of the groove on an album. When you just have someone talking, you are able to fit more grooves on the record player and thus hold more audio.

One of the greatest adaptations of the 16⅔-rpm record was a 6⅞-inch album used exclusively in Chrysler's Highway Hi-Fi car stereo system. This personalized car stereo system appeared in Chrysler automobiles from 1956–1959. The albums for this system were manufactured exclusively by Columbia Records. These records could hold approximately 45 minutes of music or up to an hour of speech per side. The Highway Hi-Fi units were factory installed with no aftermarket options. Unfortunately, the systems had a tendency to break or malfunction, so not many titles were produced. Chrysler began to pull support for the Highway Hi-Fi as early as 1957.

RCA also attempted to manufacture an automobile record player, which was available in select Chryslers. This system could stack up and play the standard 45-rpm 7-inch records. It too suffered a short lifespan due to malfunctioning.

The 16⅔-rpm speed was also utilized for records containing audiobooks, background music for businesses, and a limited number of albums. One famous label, Prestige Records, released jazz titles on 16⅔-rpm records during the 1950s. Notable releases include the Miles Davis album *Miles Davis and the Modern Jazz Giants* and the rare vinyl find *Trombone by Three*, featuring J.J. Johnson, Kai Winding, and Bennie Green. This album's cover art was created by Andy Warhol.

Vinyl Record Materials

Materials devoted to compose records have changed and evolved several times over the years. Following are some of the most common materials you'll run into as you purchase records.

Shellac

The earliest disc records produced between 1889 and 1894 were made of various materials including wax and rubber. Shortly after, a shellac-based compound became the standard material. Each manufacturer's exact formula varied, but records were typically made using cardboard and fiber, which were coated with a shellac (wax) resin. These shellac discs are not known for allowing a quiet, noise-free surface. Shellac records are commonly brittle and require careful treatment. Shellac 78s can break easily, with the remaining pieces loosely connected with the label. They can still be playable if the label holds them together, although there is a recurrent loud "pop" when passing over the crack, which can be damaging to your needle.

PVC

Following World War II, shellac supplies were exceedingly scarce, so records were sometimes pressed on a vinyl composite instead. In the 1950s–1960s, an innovative vinyl composition was broadly introduced. The composition used to fabricate vinyl records has changed and evolved over the years; however, it is primarily a blend of polyvinyl chloride (PVC). This is where the term "vinyl" was introduced.

Vinyl records are more durable and do not crack as frequently as shellac; however, they are easily scratched, and they attract a static charge, which in turn collects dust that is difficult to remove. The scratches and dust generally cause audio clicks and pops and on occasion can cause the stylus to skip. Vinyl records are easily warped by exposure to heat and improper storage and every so often have manufacturing defects.

If a record is made with partly recycled vinyl, the qual- ity suffers. For that reason, look for records that are made with virgin vinyl (meaning that they contain no recycled vinyl). Increasing the weight of the vinyl to 160–200 grams has helped avoid warping and damage. During the 1970s energy crisis, substantial petroleum shortages led to records being pressed with recycled vinyl composed of as little as 90 grams of PVC per record. The sound quality of these pressings suffered.

Colored Vinyl

Colored vinyl records have been available since as early as Edison's Amberols, which were a blue-colored shellac cylinder available between 1912 and 1929. Colored discs also appeared during the early 1900s while records were still made of shellac. Early examples include releases from Vocalion, a New York–based record label that was known for using Edison's vertical-cut method (up until 1916) and their high-quality reddish-brown shellac discs.

Between 1916 and 1949, a few other companies offered colored shellac discs, including a blue-shellacked series from Columbia during the 1930s and chocolate-colored pressings from a budget label Perfect Records prior to the 1930s.

In 1949, when RCA Victor launched its 45-rpm format, it began color-coding its records based on genre. The classifications are as follows:

- Black: pop (prefix 47)
- Green: country-western (prefix 48)
- Red: classical (prefix 49)
- Cerise (orange): R&B (prefix 50)
- Sky blue: international (prefix 51)

- Midnight blue: light classics (prefix 52)
- Opaque yellow: children's (prefix WY)

RCA only continued this practice until 1953 because it became too costly to offer these variations.

Although colored vinyl was occasionally available throughout the 1950s and 1960s, the widespread availability of colored vinyl rebounded in full force during the 1970s. During this time, the album artwork was the primary visual expression of the album, but colored discs boosted the artistic value of the entire package. Some colors that were available during the '70s included clear, transparent white, red, blue, and yellow.

COLORED VINYL SOUND QUALITY

The color of a record can slightly affect the sound quality. Black records tend to sound best, while many believe that neon, glow-in-the-dark, glitter, and splattered records sound the worst. Black vinyl has the lowest amount of surface noise, followed by standard colors, which do not require any mixing of polyvinyl.

Today, colored vinyl has grown to include almost any possible color variation. Pressing manufacturers like Erika Records in Buena Park, California, can create a record in almost any custom color. Additionally, they can create colored effects, including splatters, rainbows, swirls, and half-and-half records using just about any color combination.

Picture Discs

Picture discs, are records that feature an image visible on the playing area. They began to appear as early as the

1900s—not as discs but as square postcards with miniature records glued on the illustration. Picture discs first appeared in the 1920s, yet they did not become popular until the 1930s. The artwork on these 1930s picture-disc releases varied from images designed for the music it accompanied to film graphics and even political images with accompanying propaganda. Prior to the 1940s, the majority of picture-disc records were made of printed cardboard covered with a thin plastic, which didn't yield the best audio.

Following the end of World War II, picture discs became popular again. Vogue Records, a Detroit-based label, is noteworthy among collectors for their release of picture discs throughout the 1940s. These releases were a hit due to their attractive picture discs and quality sound. However, the appeal of these picture discs never really caught on, causing Vogue to go out of business after releasing approximately sixty-five records.

Picture discs experienced a resurgence in the 1970s through rereleases, which were used to drive up sales of highly charting albums. Some of the first modern-rock picture discs released during that time included Black Sabbath *Black Sabbath* (1974), Pink Floyd *Dark Side of the Moon* (1973), Boston *Boston* (1976), and *To Elvis: Love Still Burning* (a various artist compilation released by Pickwick Records, which is credited by *Billboard* magazine as the first picture disc to be released in the United States).

THE VOYAGER GOLDEN RECORDS
In 1977, NASA created records that contained sounds and images documenting the life and culture on Earth. These were intended for extraterrestrial life forms and were sent into outer space aboard both Voyager spacecraft.

Pickwick Records, an independent label based in Arizona, released the tribute compilation album, *To Elvis: Love Still Burning*, on an initial run of 6,000 copies, for sale through a biweekly newsletter, *The Record Digest*. After the initial release of 6,000 copies, word spread quickly and Pickwick Records had to press another 20,000 units. The success of this release showed the record industry that there was a market for picture discs.

Picture discs evolved to include shaped discs that complemented the image. Early examples include picture-disc singles such as Devo "Beautiful World," which was shaped like an astronaut head; Guns N' Roses "Nightrain," which was in the shape of a suitcase; Joe Strummer "Love Kills," shaped like a gun; and Gary Numan "Berserker," which was shaped like Gary Numan's head.

Picture discs continue to be in demand today and are still being released quite frequently. However, due to the difficult manufacturing process, picture discs tend to be a bit pricier. Even with modernized picture-disc pressings, consumers often complain about the low-quality audio on picture-disc pressings.

Flexi Discs

The flexi disc, sometimes referred to as a phonosheet or Soundsheet, is a phonograph record made from a flexible vinyl sheet. Flexi discs were created as an affordable way to include music in printed materials, such as magazines and music books. Flexi discs were introduced in 1962, when the company Eva-Tone Soundsheets patented the idea.

The use of flexi discs continued throughout the '70s and '80s, with diverse and innovative ideas. One of the more treasured flexi disc releases is The Beatles's Christmas flexi disc series. Each Christmas from 1963 through 1969, The Beatles sent out flexi discs containing messages and music to their official fan-club members. These flexi discs are popular among Beatles and other vinyl collectors, with complete sets selling for as high as over $1,000.

In addition to music, it also became common for corporations to incorporate flexi discs into their marketing. In 1988, McDonald's held a flexi disc contest that gave one lucky winner a million dollars! Chances of winning were only 1 in 80,000,000, but this campaign drew momentary attention. Flexi discs were also common additions to cereal boxes. Kids could cut out an Archie Comics disc on the back of their Super Sugar Crisp box or a Kiss flexi with their Kiss Krunch cereal. Even though flexi disc releases were mainly designed for fun and creative purposes, they are easily worn out, can warp and bend, and were not quality products.

Unusual, Obscure, and Creative Records

Over the years, obscure and unique records have been pressed using strange color combinations and unexpected materials. Here are a few memorable pressings.

X-Ray Records

During the 1950s in the Soviet Union, x-rays were used to duplicate banned music. Using x-rays discarded from hospitals, a bootlegger would cut them into circles, create a hole in the center by burning the x-ray with a cigarette, and imprint music onto the x-ray. X-ray records are highly treasured by some vinyl collectors.

Ice Record Project

To promote a single off their fourth album released in 2012, the band Shout Out Louds created ten copies of an album on ice that they sent out to select friends and press. The select group received a kit that contained a mold and bottle of water used to create the ice record. To make this record, you placed water from the bottle provided into the mold and put the mold in your freezer for a minimum of six hours. Once created, the record could be played on any turntable, giving the purchaser the opportunity to exclusively hear the debut album single before anyone else. Although ice does not project the best sound quality and could not be used for a long period of time, Shout Out Louds demonstrated it is a possible material one can use to create a record.

Laser-Etched Vinyl

Many records bear etchings, which are done on a side not containing any music. However, with a laser, an etching can be created on the grooved side of the recording and it doesn't interfere with the ability to play the music. When the album is hit by light, you can see the multicolored etching.

Liquid-Filled Records

Various pressing plants and labels have experimented with pressing different objects inside records. A few labels have experimented with pressing liquid inside a record. For Record Store Day 2012, Jack White (of The White Stripes) and his label Third Man Records released a blue-liquid-filled version of his single "Sixteen Saltines." While you play the vinyl, you can gaze at the blue water swooshing around inside the record. The band Worthless released a limited edition of only fifteen liquid-filled records for their single "Greener Grass" (shortly after, they did an additional run of fifty copies). These liquid-filled records were created by the artist Curtis Godino.

In 2016, Mondo, an arts-based company out of Austin, Texas, that is famous within the vinyl community for their elaborate soundtrack record releases, announced the release of a liquid-filled *Aliens* soundtrack that is filled with green Xenomorph "blood." The record release coincided with 20th Century Fox's declaration of April 26 as Alien Day. This liquid-filled record was limited to only seventy-five copies and was also handcrafted by artist Curtis Godino.

Blood-Filled Record

In 2012, The Flaming Lips released a human blood–filled version of their album *The Flaming Lips and Heady Fwends*. Blood samples were collected from various contributors to the album, including Chris Martin (Coldplay), Alan Palomo (Neon Indian), Erykah Badu, New Fumes, Kesha, Justin Vernon (Bon Iver), Alex Ebert and Stewart Cole (Edward Sharpe and the Magnetic Zeros), Jim James (My Morning Jacket), Brian Gibson and Brian Chippendale (Lightning Bolt), and Sean Lennon and Charlotte Kemp Muhl (The Ghost of a Saber Tooth Tiger). Only ten copies were ever made and were available for sale at a price of $2,500, with all proceeds going to the Oklahoma Humane Society and the Academy of Contemporary Music.

Records Filled with Other Things

For a 2014 Record Store Day exclusive, the band Liars released a two-disc special edition of their album *Mess*. One of the discs has colored string pressed into clear vinyl. Only 500 copies were made, and each album has a unique string placement.

In 2014, the band Barren Harvest pressed a limited run of their album *Subtle Cruelties* that contained leaves pressed in the center of the record. These were limited to 100 copies and were manufactured by Pirates Press.

British company And Vinyly offers a service allowing you to press cremated ashes of a loved one into a 12-inch clear vinyl, which can contain music or any sort of audio that you choose. The cost of pressing ashes into vinyl starts at about $2,700 (£2,000) for thirty discs.

CHAPTER 2

How Records Are Made

a lthough the production of phonographic records saw many developments during its first sixty years, the process of how a record is pressed today has not changed drastically since the 1940s.

An Overview

Essentially, pressing a record can be broken down into these five steps:

1. Record the sound
2. Create a lacquer
3. Create a master stamper
4. Press and approve test pressing
5. Press the record using an extruder and pressing machine

The first step in making a record, producing the actual recording of the music, is the step that has seen the most significant advancement over the last seventy years. After the master recording is perfected, one must produce a master disc. To do so, a lathe is applied to cut the master recording onto a lacquer. At this stage, the lacquer is utilized to create a mother stamper. Next, pressing stampers are made. The pressing stampers generate test pressings that are spun by the record label to assure that the quality of the record is up to par before the records are manufactured. After the album is quality controlled and approved, the record is made using a record-pressing machine.

Sounds simple, right? Not exactly. In the following sections, each step is explained in detail along with a description of the issues that may occur during this process.

Record the Sound

The sound-recording process has progressed in waves as technological advancements have been introduced. The way sound is recorded can be divided into four particular periods:

Acoustic Era (1877–1925)

The acoustic era began with Edison's phonograph creation. The first recordings were made using mechanical recorders, often a large conical horn. These recordings were limited in frequency range and volume. There was only one conical horn, which was the recording medium utilized to pick up *all* the sounds. That made balancing the sound a challenge, usually achieved through experimentation. A performer's position near the horn was based on how strongly the sound recorded. The stronger the sound, the further away it was moved from the horn; quieter sounds were moved closer to the horn. During this era, the sound was all recorded live, so there were many limitations on the outcome of the recordings.

Electrical Era (1925–1945)

The electrical era came about with the introduction of Western Electric's system that included electrical microphones, electronic signal amplifiers, and electric disc-cutting machines. This allowed sound to be captured, amplified, filtered, and balanced electronically.

Magnetic Era (1945–1975)

Magnetic tape recording was invented in the 1930s, but was a German invention restricted to Germany. Following World War II, Allied nations had access to this invention. They found that the quality of audio that was prerecorded on magnetic tape was equivalent to live broadcasts, and it quickly became an industry standard.

With the ability to no longer be restricted to recording live, the use of magnetic tape led to the use of multitrack tape recording. The sound captured on tape could be manipulated and edited. This allowed for a fresh, sophisticated sound within pop music.

Digital Era (1975–Present)

Digital recording began around 1975, but the first digitally recorded pop album was not released until 1979 (Ry Cooder *Bop Till You Drop*). Quickly following this, digital recording became the industry standard.

The majority of currently pressed vinyl uses "digitally recorded masters." That means that even if an album was originally recorded during the magnetic era on tape, a mastering studio creates a digital master from the original tape that is later provided to the lacquer cutter.

Sound Playback

How sound is played back on a turntable has seen three significant developments affecting how audio is heard—mono, stereo, and quad. Before you make a vinyl record, you need to choose which type of playback audio you'll use to make it.

Monophonic Sound (Mono)

Prior to 1931, sound reproduction was monophonic, meaning that sound was heard as if it was coming from a single position, often referred to as a single channel. With mono recordings, only one speaker is required because all the audio signals are mixed together and are outputted through a single audio channel, typically a speaker or head-phones. If mono sound is played through multiple speak-ers or headphones, an identical signal is fed through each speaker. Many releases prior to the 1960s were recorded and mixed in monophonic format.

Stereophonic Sound (Stereo)

Generally known as "stereo," stereophonic sound re-produces audio in a way that creates depth. When you experience a live musical performance with multiple band members, they are positioned in such a way that their instru-ments complement each other. When at a concert, audio is reaching you from many directions, not one direction as it does with mono recordings. Stereophonic sound is created by using two or more audio channels through two or more speakers, allowing you to hear different sounds from differ-ent speakers, which creates a more authentic experience. Al-though stereophonic sound had been demonstrated in the nineteenth century, it wasn't patented until 1831 (by Alan Blumlein). Stereo records are still prevalent today.

According to a *Billboard* article, Audio Fidelity Records, a company based out of New York City, was the first to mass-produce an American stereophonic long-playing record. On Friday, December 13, 1957, Audio Fidelity introduced to the public a demonstration disc that featured six tracks from the Dukes of Dixieland on side one and steam and diesel rail-road sound effects on side two. This release, catalog num-ber AFLP 1872, was only ever pressed on 500 copies, which were given to people within the record industry. In that same issue of *Billboard*, Audio Fidelity advertised that, as a service to the industry, it would provide any accredited members of the record industry, upon request on company letterhead, a free copy of this recording. This album is extremely rare and hard to find.

Quadraphonic Sound (Quad)

During the 1970s, quadraphonic sound, which uses four channels instead of two (similar to 4.0 surround sound), was introduced. Quadraphonic sound was never a commercial success within the vinyl market because the equipment required to play quadraphonic records was costly. Quadraphonic records can be played with a regular, stereo two-channel turntable and speaker setup; however, you will not be able to experience the quadraphonic sound. Although quadraphonic sound did not dominate in the mass market, there are quite a few titles and a niche collectors' market.

QUADRAPHONIC RECORDS
Although quadraphonic records did not take off, many quadraphonic titles are highly sought after by collectors, with many titles selling for hundreds, even thousands of dollars. Coveted quadraphonic titles include The Taj Mahal Travellers *July 15, 1972*, Krokodil *Sweat and Swim*, Pink Floyd *Dark Side of the Moon*, and various Elvis Presley titles.

Creating the Lacquer

Once you have recorded audio, the next step is to begin the duplication process by making a lacquer. To create a lacquer, you essentially take a master recording, whether it is a digital recording, a magnetic tape, or another medium, and record that audio onto a lacquer using a lathe. A lacquer, occasionally referred to as an acetate, consists of an aluminum disc core that is coated with black lacquer. (The term *acetate* originates from the material contained within master disc cuts before 1934—cellulose acetate. Cellulose acetate is no longer in use.)

The actual creation of the lacquer disc is a bit tedious.

1. First, an aluminum disc runs through a machine, coating it with the nitrocellulose lacquer, a substance similar to nail polish.
2. Rollers with scrapers remove the runoff and excess lacquer from the disc, and the surplus lacquer is caught in a basin for reuse.
3. The disc hardens fairly quickly, similar to nail polish. Often during this process, flaws can appear. During the quality-control stage, lacquers with pits, bumps, or dirt are discarded and recycled.
4. Discs that pass the quality-control stage are placed under a hole puncher and a hole is punched into the center.
5. The lacquer is at that point packaged carefully and shipped off to the engineer.

The lacquer disc is a precisely smooth disc with no grooves. The audio is placed onto the lacquer by cutting grooves into the disc using a recording machine called a lathe. The engineer places the disc onto the lathe's platter and positions a microscope and cutter to the edge of the disc. Once ready to record, he begins the audio and the lathe begins cutting the grooves. Lathes bear either a ruby or sapphire cutting head.

When the recording is concluded, the disc is inspected, and if approved, an etching containing a serial number chosen by the record label is etched onto the matrix area (the area at the end of the record between the end of the grooves and the center area). The lacquer is now sent off to generate the impression.

Plating

To create the actual stampers for the purpose of pressing the record, manufacturers first must produce plates. To create the plates, the lacquer disc is washed and sprayed with tin chloride and liquid silver. The tin chloride assists the silver in adhering to the lacquer. Then the disc is washed again to get rid of any extra bits of liquid silver that did not stick. Next, a duller silver metal is added to stiffen the disc and prepare it for the final step.

FOR MORE ON LACQUER AND PLATING
For those interested in the lacquer and plating cutting process, check out The Secret Society of Lathe Trolls, an online community of vinyl engineers who work in the lacquer and plating industry: www.lathetrolls.com.

At this step, the disc is fastened to a spindle of a tank lid. The disc spins and the disc is rinsed an additional time. The spinning disc is then placed into a bath solution containing nickel nuggets. An electric charge fuses the nickel to the silver. Once complete, the lacquer is removed from the tank and the nickel layer is pried away from the disc. The layer of nickel is now a stamper and the lacquer is discarded. A center hole is punched into the stamper disc. A cutting wheel trims the disc to the finished product's sizing specs. The stampers are now ready to use for making vinyl records.

Test Pressings

When the stampers are ready, the pressing plant will run a small number of records, usually ranging from five to twenty copies, called test pressings. The process of creating test pressings is exactly the same as making the record (see the following section).

Test pressings are reviewed by the manufacturing plant, and if their quality is approved, they are provided to the record label, artists, and on occasion the mastering engineers. It is essential for the record label to thoroughly review any test-pressing issues before approving and mass-producing the album.

When listening to a test pressing it is critical to first clean the test pressing. This assures that any dust, dirt, or static

NOT ALL RECORDS PLAY FROM THE OUTER EDGE
Many classical long-play records were cut from the center of the record. The outer edge of a record can fit a longer groove, which was better suited for loud-sounding finales. The improved sound quality of the outer edge is also one of the main reasons why signature tracks are placed on or near the beginning of an album.

that it may have attracted while in transit is removed. Next, a test pressing should be inspected for any visual issues such as scratches, warping, or an off-center label or center hole. While listening to a test pressing, musicians and engineers review the audio in detail several times to assure there are no issues such as pops, clicks, a whooshing sound, or skips.

The audio should sound the same as the master audio, without any additional unwanted noise.

If any visual or audio issues are encountered during this process, the staff will check other test pressings to see if the issue is present on all discs. For example, if anyone hears a pop and then discovers a scratch in the area on the disc where the audio pops, the group will review all other discs to confirm if they have the same defect. A scratch can occur while in transit, so if it is not present on the other test pressings, it may not be a pressing issue. If it is present on all discs, it likely is a manufacturing issue and could be present on all records.

Pressing a Record

Once the test pressing is approved, it is time to duplicate the discs. The first step to pressing a record is to prepare the center labels. Center labels need to be dried in an oven before being applied to a record. This step helps eliminate some of the moisture within the center label inks. Next, a machine cuts a hole within a stack of center labels. The labels are placed on a mini press that rounds out the labels. The center labels are now ready to be pressed onto the records.

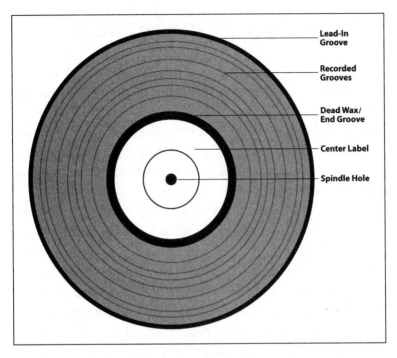

Lead-In Groove

Recorded Grooves

Dead Wax/ End Groove

Center Label

Spindle Hole

Parts of a vinyl record.

The polyvinyl pellets, the material needed to mold a record, are now poured into a hopper. The pellets fall from this hopper into an extruder, which heats them into a hot rubber patty called a puck or biscuit. Hoists attached above and below place the center labels on and suction cups hold them in place. The biscuit is moved forward and placed on the press between the two stampers. The stamper applies 100 tons of pressure while heated to approximately 374°F. The pellets are next melted and molded into the record, creating the grooves. A quick cooling cycle hardens it and bonds the labels to the record. The record is sent to the trimming table where it cuts away the excess edges. The record is then placed on a stack and cooled. Once cooled, you have a finished record.

The Problems with Current Machinery

During the 1980s, when vinyl record sales began to tank, the manufacturing of modern pressing machines halted. That's why pressing machines currently operational within pressing plants are at least thirty years old. They generally require a great deal of upkeep, yet they still break down and are costly to repair. The recent huge demand for vinyl has taxed these already aging machines.

The second hurdle with these older machines is the average cycle time to press a record ranges from 40 to 90 seconds, making the total output per machine fairly low. With today's vinyl boom the highest in decades, record-pressing companies are not able to keep up with the demand thanks to their slow production and cycle times, outdated machines, and inability to find needed machines and parts. Prior to the vinyl boom, pressing plants had an average turnaround time of about 2–6 weeks (after test pressings are approved). By 2015, record labels experienced turnaround times of 4–6 months (after test pressings are approved) and they still hover around this extensive wait time today.

New Machines on the Market

At the end of 2015, the first newly produced pressing machines were announced. Newbilt Machinery, a company based in Germany, introduced a new machine that is a cloned but updated design of the Finebilt, a popular and reliable old machine numerous pressing plants still use. The Newbilt system is a single or duplex manual press, which includes an extruder and a record-trimming machine. Improvements from the Finebilt to the Newbilt include improved performance and durability on their machines. They have also decreased the cycle time on their duplex system.

In early 2016, a second company, Viryl Technologies, announced the creation of a contemporary record-pressing machine called the WarmTone. This is a completely modernized, fully automatic machine promising accelerated cycle times, reduced power consumption, and less wasted PVC. With faster pressing cycles, the WarmTone is expected to significantly improve the extreme wait times that record-manufacturing plants currently experience.

Vinyl Record Jackets and Artwork

The final step to creating a record is packaging it. While it may seem odd to think of now, early records didn't have the elaborate artwork we expect today.

Early Packaging

Early cylinder records were encased in cylinder rolls comparable to a film canister. Disc records during this time and up until the early 1900s were typically stored in brown or cardboard sleeves made out of acid paper, which were occasionally printed on but usually left blank. These sleeves did not preserve well. Typically, the sleeves had a hole cut out of the center so that the center label was visible. By the early 1920s, collections of bound sleeves with a paper or leather cover were sold as record albums. These could be stored upright on a shelf, protecting the records.

Enter the Cover Art

During the 1930s, records were still primarily sold in plain packaging with the exception of special collections featuring one performer or a single genre of music, which were sold in colorful packaging. In 1938, Columbia Records hired Alex Steinweiss as their art director. During his employment there, he essentially invented album cover art. Alex designed approximately 2,500 record covers from 1938 up until he semi-iretired in 1971.

COVER ART DESIGNERS

In the old days, being awarded the opportunity to design a cover was a coveted accolade for artists. The importance of album cover design was so significant that many artists gained prominence through the covers they designed. Herb Alpert and the Tijuana Brass's 1965 release *Whipped Cream & Other Delights* has sold more than 6 million copies, which is often credited to its cover art. The cover was racy for its time, featuring model Dolores Erickson wearing chiffon and whipped cream. To date, this album is so iconic that in addition to it being a key record to collect, it has also inspired numerous parodies.

After Columbia's introduction of artistically designed covers, it quickly became a crucial cultural part of the music experience. During the 1950s, the gatefold (an extra panel that folds open) was introduced as a way to offer added art as opposed to a standard LP jacket. Gatefolds became quite popular, especially with progressive rock during the 1960s and 1970s. When folded, a gatefold album is the same size as a standard LP cover, but when opened like a book it's approximately 24 inches in length and 12½ inches tall, doubling the amount of space available for art.

Over the years, releases became progressively visionary while encompassing additional art components such as inserts, posters, printed record sleeves, lyrics, photos, drawings, and more. Fans were given a total audio-visual experience where they were able to pair visual art to the audio sounds they experienced. If you love album art, check out a documentary titled *The Cover Story*, which interviews various artists and industry executives about cover art.

Now that you are up to speed on vinyl history and production, let's get you out there buying a turntable!

CHAPTER 3

Turntables 101

In order for audio to be heard from a record, certain key equipment is required—the turntable, amplifier, and speakers. Creating a turntable setup in your own home is a fairly simple process. Throughout this chapter, I'll explain each of these pieces of equipment. You'll also find tips to make sure you avoid rookie mistakes as you set up your turntable. Lastly, you'll learn a bit of maintenance for keeping your turntable in tiptop condition for years to come.

Anatomy of a Turntable

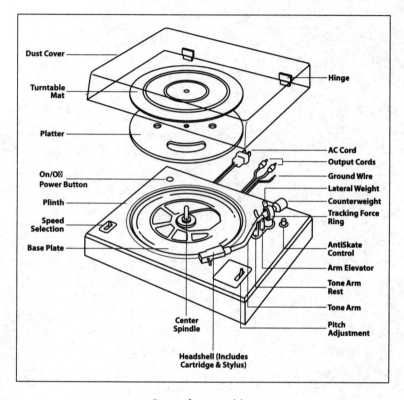

Parts of a turntable.

Several of the following components are present on every turntable, and others are features available with certain models. Following is a breakdown of basic turntable anatomy:

Plinth

This is the base of the turntable, which is used for support and to conceal all the mechanisms inside the turntable. A quality plinth is built with solid materials that support the turntable and were chosen specifically by the manufacturer

based on how they affect the audio output. Typical materi-
als used when building a quality plinth include solid wood, metal, and high-quality MDF. Some high-quality turntables are equipped with a dual-plinth base, which separates some of the electrical parts of the turntable from the top plinth, eliminating any unwanted noise those components may create when a record is playing.

Dust Cover

This is a hinged lid that is typically translucent, which you open and close over the turntable. Typically, you place your turntable dust cover down when your turntable is not spinning records.

Start/Stop Button

Allows you to start or stop the platter from spinning.

Platter

This is where you place the record. It is a round disc that spins the record clockwise at the desired rpm. Different manufacturers employ distinctive materials for their platters, including aluminum, acrylic, glass, or plastic, all with the belief that their selected material best affects the output of the sound quality. Many audiophiles prefer an acrylic platter, which can be purchased as an aftermarket upgrade for certain turntables. Acrylic platters don't need a turntable mat and will drastically improve the sound quality.

Slip Mat/Turntable Mat

A slip mat and turntable mat are circular pieces of material that you place on the platter to grip the record. The DJ slip mat's primary function is to allow DJs to smoothly move and manipulate the record while it's playing, while a turntable mat holds the record in place.

Center Spindle

The center spindle fastens the record in place and holds it there while the album spins. You place the hole in the vinyl record over this spindle.

Turntable Weight

This attaches to your center spindle and can be used to hold down the record tight to the platter.

Stylus

The stylus is the needle that touches the record grooves during play. The stylus is held inside a cartridge. It is rated to work properly for a certain number of hours, typically 2,000–3,000 playing hours. Styluses are typically either made from diamond or sapphire and can be either elliptical or spherical shaped. Spherical styluses are cheaper to produce and therefore are the most common. The elliptical stylus can follow the groove more accurately, providing a higher-quality sound.

Cartridge

The cartridge is what holds the stylus in place. The cartridge converts the movement of the stylus into a signal that is fed to your phono output and then to the amplifier and speakers, where they are converted into sound. Cartridges are available in both ceramic and magnetic. Ceramic cartridges are typically found with inexpensive, portable record players. Magnetic cartridges are most commonly used and typically what you find included with a quality turntable.

There are three primary types of magnetic cartridges available:

1. **Moving magnet (MM):** In a moving-magnet cartridge, the stylus carries a tiny permanent magnet positioned at the end of the stylus cantilevered between two sets of fixed coils, one for the left audio channel and one for the right. The magnet vibrates while the stylus follows the record groove, and it prompts a tiny current in the coils.

2. **Moving iron (MI):** This is essentially the same design as a moving-magnet cartridge, with the iron replacing the magnet that sits on the stylus cantilever.

3. **Moving coil (MC):** With moving-coil cartridges, the coils are attached to the stylus and move within the field of a fixed magnet. This is basically the reverse design of a moving magnet. If a tiny coil is used due to the lack of space, then the moving-coil cartridge is considered to be "low output." In addition to a preamp, low-output moving-coil cartridges require an additional amplification stage or a step-up transponder. High-output moving-coil cartridges are also available, but do not require this additional amplification.

Headshell

A headshell holds the cartridge and stylus in place and connects the stylus and cartridge to the tone arm.

Tone Arm

The tone arm holds the headshell, stylus, and cartridge in place. It also controls the stylus and assures it moves through the record groove smoothly. Some turntables have a straight tone arm, while others have curved tone arms. Some people believe that curved tone arms produce a superior sound because the S shape makes the arm fit better within smaller areas on the record, creating less tracking error.

Tone Arm Rest

A contraption that allows you to securely fasten your tone arm when the turntable is not in use. It is imperative to rest the tone arm here when your turntable is not spinning records to avoid potential damage.

Speed Selection

Allows you to change the speed (rpm) that the turntable plays. Two-speed turntables play both 33⅓ and 45 rpm. Three-speed turntables offer 33⅓, 45, and 78 rpm speeds. Select vintage turntables offer four speeds: 33⅓, 45, 78, and 16⅔ rpm.

Cueing Lever

Manual turntables often include a cueing lever, which assists with gentle dropping and lifting of the stylus onto the record. With a cueing lever you can position the tone arm above the point on the record you wish the stylus to land on, and then use the cueing lever to gently drop the stylus. When the record is done, you use the cueing lever to remove the stylus from the record before manually placing it back in its place.

Counterweight

The counterweight allows you to control the amount of pressure the stylus applies to the record, which affects the overall output of the sound. Numerous budget-priced turntables, such as the Crosley Cruiser, don't include a counterweight. But from experience, I have noticed that if you don't have a counterweight, you will occasionally have trouble keeping the stylus within the grooves of the record, which in turn creates extreme pops, skips, and skating (when the stylus slides over the record incorrectly). Later in this chapter, you'll learn how to balance a tone arm, which includes setting your counterweight, because having an effectively balanced tone arm is extremely important.

Antiskate Control

This is a control feature on select turntables that helps the stylus move smoothly through the center of the groove. The force applied from a rotating record tends to draw the tone arm toward the center of the record and from time to time can cause the needle to skip across the grooves, referred to as skating. This distorts the balance of sound and causes wear and tear on the tone arm. The antiskate control is a feature that allows you to adjust how much force is applied to the tone arm to avoid skating.

Pitch Adjustment

This feature is only included on professional turntables so that DJs can beat match, the act of slowing down or increasing the speed of one playing record to match the tempo of an upcoming record to create a seamless transition between tracks. The pitch adjustment feature adjusts the speed of the platter within a certain range, measured in percentages. Different turntables offer different settings, and they typically ranges from as low as +/- 8% to as high as +/- 50%.

Strobe Light

The strobe light feature is not available on all turntables. The strobe light is primarily used by DJs to beat match and to verify that the platter is spinning at the exact desired rpm.

Here's how a strobe light works on a Technics SL-1200 turntable, widely used by DJs and recently reintroduced into the market. The Technics turntable has four rows of lights on the outside of the platter: The two top rows have smaller-sized dots, the dots within the third row are larger, and the dots in the fourth row are the same small size as in rows one and two. If your platter is spinning at the exact rpm you have selected, the larger, third row of dots within the strobe pattern will light up but not appear to move. If you are utilizing a pitch adjustment to increase or decrease the speed, the larger and small dots will move at different speeds and can be used to gauge the approximate percentage the pitch has been adjusted.

So when your pitch control is set to zero, you want to see stationary large dots. If the large dots are not stationary, this could indicate an issue with your motor or pitch control.

Phono Output Cord

These are the cables that transfer the audio from your turntable to your preamp (or receiver if a preamp is not required). Cables used are either a phono connection or RCA. RCA connections are the white, red, and yellow prongs you typically see on electronic devices.

Power Cable and Ground Wire

The power cable simply plugs the turntable into your power supply. The ground wire, sometimes referred to as an earth wire, is a skinny wire that is plugged into a screw or post (often marked "ground") on the preamp or receiver. The purpose of this wire is to prevent a ground loop that diverts feedback, in turn creating an audible humming noise.

Built-In Preamp

A turntable outputs a very low phono signal, so it must be boosted either by the receiver or by a preamp (if the receiver doesn't have a phono input) before you can hear the sound through the speakers. Some turntables include their own built-in preamp, which means they can hook up to a receiver or speakers directly without the use of a separate preamp. Select turntables allow you to bypass the built-in preamp, allowing you to either use the preamp provided or add your own.

USB Port

Purchasing a turntable with a USB port will allow you to plug your turntable directly into your computer. This will allow you to record the audio from your turntable to your computer as well as use your computer setup as speakers.

Other Turntable Terminology

Beyond these basic components are the machinery that make a turntable work. You'll see these terms in descriptions of various models when you shop.

Belt Drive versus Direct Drive versus Idler Wheel

Turntables are commonly classified as either belt drive, direct drive, or idler wheel. These three names refer to the way the platter and the motor are connected.

BELT-DRIVEN

Belt-driven turntables have their motor located off center from the platter, typically underneath or completely outside of it. The platter is connected to the motor with a belt, made of an elastic material employed to absorb motor vibrations. Belt-drive turntables are generally believed to produce good sound quality because the motor is isolated from the platter, which results in less noise being transmitted to the tone arm.

Drawbacks to a belt-driven turntable include wear and tear from the elasticity on the belt and their inability to play the record at full rpm instantaneously, which creates a slurring sound as the motor starts up. However, the time it does require to rev up to speed is only one second, and wear and tear on belts does not occur for several years.

DIRECT DRIVE

Direct-drive turntables have their motor located directly under the center of the platter, connected directly to the platter. Direct-drive turntables offer consistent speeds and have a higher torque than belt-driven turntables, meaning the platter will accelerate to its desired speed faster than belt-driven turntables.

As a result of the motor being close to the platter, possible vibration from the proximity of this motor to the platter can be a drawback. In recent years, turntable manufacturers have added shock-absorbing materials to make this less of a problem.

IDLER WHEEL

You'll usually find idler-wheel connections on turntables made before the 1970s. An idler-wheel turntable utilizes a rubber tire to couple the motor to the turntable platter. These systems tended to introduce a low-frequency "rumble" in addition to a "wow" created by speed variations.

Manual versus Automatic

Manual and automatic operation refer to how the tone arm is moved to and from its starting position. With a fully automatic turntable, you simply press a button that begins the spinning of the motor, and the tone arm automatically lifts and places the stylus on the record at the lead-in groove to begin playing the record. Once the album is complete, the tone arm will lift and move back into its starting position.

Manual turntables require you to move the tone arm yourself or with the help of a cueing lever. You usually press a button to begin the platter spinning, and then you physically move the tone arm to place the stylus on the record. Once the record has finished playing, you physically return the tone arm back to its starting position. If your turntable includes a cueing lever, physically move the tone arm over the record to the approximate spot you want it to land on the record and use the cueing lever to move it down onto the record.

Although automatic turntables have the benefit of easily starting a stopped record, audiophiles argue that the addition of the gears and parts needed to operate the automatic function interferes with a turntable's sound quality. On the flip side, many people dislike manual turntables because when the side of your record is complete, you must stand up and stop the platter from spinning and then move the needle back to its resting place. Not removing the stylus when your record is complete will cause wear and tear to your stylus.

Tracking Force

The tracking force is the amount of weight the stylus applies to the record while spinning. A good turntable will allow you to adjust the tracking force. This is also referred to as "balancing the tone arm" on higher-end turntables.

Balancing the tone arm allows you to adjust the amount of weight that your stylus applies to the record while it spins.

Torque

Torque is the measure of how strong the motor on a turntable causes the platter to rotate. Direct-drive turntables tend to have heavier torque because the motor is located underneath the platter, allowing it to spin up to the desired speed faster.

Wow/Flutter

Wow/flutter is an audible effect that occurs on record players, cassette players, and other analog equipment with rotary components such as a turntable. When referring to turntables, the wow/flutter percentage tells you the percentage the platter's rpm will fluctuate while it spins. A lower wow/flutter percentage represents a higher-quality motor because you are less likely to notice any audible inconsistencies. Most new turntables have a wow/flutter between 0.10% and 0.25%. For the average listener, a wow/flutter below 0.20% will likely produce no discernable audible differences.

The Preamp

The output signal produced by a turntable is phono, which is a quiet signal that requires amplification in order to be heard at a reasonable volume. Although turntables are made using a phono signal, the speakers and receiver you are likely to use are at a line level. A phono signal requires additional amplification in order to work properly with a line-level stereo system. If a preamp is not included within a turntable, the audio will sound muted and inaudible. A phono preamp is used to convert the phono audio to line level, giving it the ability to be amplified at a louder sound.

The good news is that preamps are very versatile—they can be built into the turntable, receiver, or added to your setup as a standalone piece. If you buy a new turntable with a USB output, it will include a built-in preamp. Additionally, select vintage and newly manufactured receivers include built-in preamps that have a "PHONO" marking on them.

If you already have a receiver set up for a stereo or surround sound that does not have a phono input and you choose a turntable that requires a preamp, you should probably purchase a phono preamp to avoid having to buy a different receiver and speakers. Phono preamps range in cost from $50 to over $500. Phono preamps play a critical role in the quality of your audio output, and purchasing a higher-quality (and unfortunately more expensive) preamp will increase the capability of your setup. However, preamps are a component of your turntable setup that can be upgraded or changed in the future. Therefore, if you are on a budget, you can purchase a lower-priced individual preamp or a receiver with one built in and upgrade to a more expensive, higher-quality preamp down the road.

A word of caution: many audiophiles advise against built-in preamps because they think that having additional components near the motor creates added unwanted noise. Additionally, the preamps that are built within a turntable are often poor quality compared to those within a receiver or purchased as a completely separate component. Here are a range of preamps to consider:

- Pro-Ject Audio Phono Box (MM, MC; $79.99)

- Bellari VP130 Tube Phono Preamp ($275)
- Clearaudio Nano V2 ($450)
- Pro-Ject Audio Tube Box DS ($699.99)

Receiver

You will likely need to buy a receiver for your setup because this is the component that transmits the sound from the turntable to the speakers. The receiver either needs to be used in addition to a preamp, or you can buy a receiver that includes a built-in phono preamp. Although purchasing a turntable with a built-in preamp is frowned upon by audiophiles, purchasing a quality receiver with a built-in preamp does not affect the audio output to a huge degree. Here are some receiver terms and considerations you should be aware of before you purchase one:

1. **Receiver inputs:** Make sure the receiver you buy includes a phono input (if you don't have or require a preamp) or an audio input for your turntable, typically connected with RCA cables, plus enough inputs (and of the correct type, e.g., HDMI, digital, optical) for whatever other components you might want to connect to your receiver.
2. **Power requirements:** Receivers can produce various amounts of power. Typical home setups do not require a huge amount of power; however, if you intend to connect several devices to your receiver (such as a TV or a stereo), ask your electronics dealer to assure the receiver will provide sufficient power.
3. **Size and dimensions:** Make sure the receiver is an appropriate size to fit within the setup you select. Receivers can range from 14 to more than 20 inches

deep and anywhere from 10 to 17 inches wide. Be sure to bring along with you a measurement of the space you have available.

4. **Multichannel:** If you expect to use your receiver for other devices such as surround sound, purchase a receiver with five or seven channels as opposed to the two channels standard stereo receivers provide.

5. **Warranty:** All new receivers should come with a warranty or return policy.

Here are some reputable receivers that include built-in preamps in a variety of price ranges:

- Onkyo TX-8020 ($159)
- Yamaha R-S300 ($279)
- Marantz Integrated Amplifier PM5005 ($499)

Here are some high-quality receivers that do not include built-in preamps:

- Yamaha R-S201 ($179.99)
- Yamaha RX-V479 ($299.99)
- Harman Kardon AVR 1610S ($399)
- Harman Kardon AVR 3700 ($399)
- Denon AVR-S920W ($529)

Speakers

Speakers are the piece of the turntable setup that will reproduce the final sound; therefore, purchasing a quality pair of speakers is essential to get the best sound out of your turntable. Whether you buy a new or vintage turntable, doing a bit of research on what speakers to pair with your turntable will go a long way.

Speakers are available in a variety of shapes and sizes. The space where you will have your turntable set up will likely control what type of speaker you buy. You can select from the following types:

- **Floor speakers:** Larger, standing speakers that are placed on the floor. Since they are sizable, encased speakers, they require no additional support or stand and are effortless to include in your setup, if you have the space. You can drop some serious money on audiophile-quality floor-standing speakers (the highly rated PSB Imagine T3 sells for $3,750/speaker), but if you don't have a pile of money burning a hole in your pocket, check out these models: Pioneer SP-FS52-LR, $129/speaker; Polk Audio RTi A5, $399/speaker; Klipsch R-28F, $449/speaker; Klipsch RF-7, $1,599/speaker. Be aware that prices for most floor-standing speakers are given per speaker, so you'll have to double the price quoted for a pair.
- **Bookshelf speakers:** Smaller-scale speakers that sit on a shelf or a speaker stand. If you do not have a way to incorporate a shelving unit to hold these speakers, you can buy separate stands so you can position one speaker to the right and and one to the left of your turntable. You can spend anywhere from under $100 to over $1,000 for a pair of bookshelf speakers. Some models you might want to look at include Dayton Audio B652-AIR, $49/pair; Pioneer SP-BS22-LR, $129/pair; Elac Debut B6, the top pick from The Wirecutter website, $279/pair; Dali Zensor 3, $595/pair; and the KEF R300, $1,799/pair.

- **Ceiling/in-wall speakers:** Tiny speakers that mount on a wall or are installed flush to a ceiling. Here are a few suggested models: Premier Acoustic PA-626 ($212.50); Polk Audio RC65i ($449+); and the Klipsch In-Wall or In-Ceiling Speakers (between $1,000–$2,000).
- **Soundbar:** A soundbar is a long, narrow speaker enclosure utilizing a line-array setup or multiple drivers that usually sits in front of a TV, but it can be used with a turntable setup. Some soundbars are packaged with a separate subwoofer. It provides decent sound; however, it is not recommended if you are aiming for a higher-end, audiophile setup. Here are some models to check out: Vizio SB3821-C6, $158; Yamaha YAS-105, with built-in subwoofer, $249; and Yamaha YAS-203, with external subwoofer, $399.
- **Active speakers:** Also known as powered speakers, they are speakers that have built-in amplifiers and can be connected directly to a turntable without a receiver. Active speakers always include a power source. Some models include a built-in preamp and some require a preamp to be added. Models to consider include: Audioengine A2+ ($249.99); Kanto YUMI ($299.99); and Klipsch R-15PM ($499.99).

Now that you have an understanding of the basic components needed for a turntable setup (preamp, receiver, and speakers), let's explore the nitty-gritty about purchasing a turntable!

CHAPTER 4

Purchasing a Turntable

n ow that you understand the components of a turntable, you can start to think about purchasing one. With so many options on the market today, it's important to first figure out exactly how and where you'll use your turntable—and your budget.

70 What Are Your Needs?

The first question you must ask yourself is how you intend to use the turntable you purchase.

- Do you want to become the next hot club DJ and therefore need features such as pitch control and a direct-drive turntable (the optimal choice for scratching)?
- Are you aiming to become an an audiophile, looking to achieve a high-fidelity sound reproduction?
- Do you just want a simple setup that produces quality audio and is painless for others in your household to also enjoy?

Whatever your needs may be, you'll find several options within all price ranges.

Prior to heading out and purchasing a turntable, you must have an idea as to where you wish to set up your turntable. If you have flexibility with where your turntable will be placed, choose wisely. Frequently, people prefer to have their setup incorporated within their living room or family room, allowing their vinyl hobby to be a communal experience. Avid record collectors may desire to dedicate an entire bedroom, basement, or garage as their collections are large and the amount of time they invest in listening to records may interfere with others in their household. Additionally, you will need a place to house your receiver, a sturdy table or shelf to sit your turntable on, and space for your speakers. Understanding and planning your turntable setup ahead of time will allow you to better decide what type of turntable, amplifier/receiver, and speakers you select.

The following sections explore a variety of turntable models; both new and used are favored within various budgets. This will provide you with a sense of both what you can at-

tain within your budget in addition to what features to look
for when purchasing a turntable.

Turntable Setup Components

Here are a few typical setup options:

- Turntable with built-in preamp and active speakers: Best for those looking for a simple, easy-to-use setup.
- Turntable, receiver with built-in preamp, and speakers: Best for the occasional vinyl user.
- Turntable, separate preamp, and active speakers: Best for the occasional vinyl user (see the following illustration, top).
- Turntable, preamp, receiver, and speakers: Best for the occasional vinyl user (see the following illustration, bottom).

We'll look at each of those parts in more detail in the rest of the chapter.

Buying a Used or Vintage Turntable

One of the benefits to purchasing a vintage turntable is that you can acquire a high-quality turntable without the high cost. They do require some research ahead of time, though. If you are fairly familiar and interested in electronics, your search can be a fun and rewarding experience. If you do not have an interest or an aptitude for electronics, a new turntable may be the best route, especially considering they are available within all budgets.

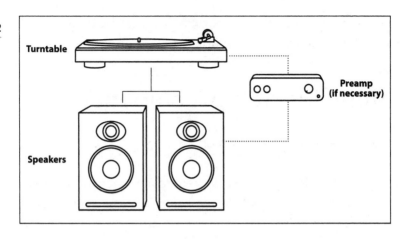

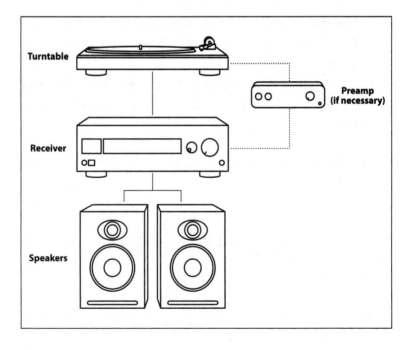

Whether purchasing a used turntable in person or online, here is a list of basic questions you can ask to ascertain a turntable's condition:

- Is the turntable currently with its original owner?
- Have there been any functionality issues?
- How many hours per week was the turntable used?
- Has it ever been used by a DJ?
- Are all the pieces included, or have any of them gone missing or broken over the years? (For example, the stylus, dust cover, slip mat, manual, original box, etc.)
- If the cartridge and stylus are included, how long has that cartridge or stylus been on the turntable?
- Does the turntable have all its original components or have any been replaced?
- If a belt-driven turntable, is the belt in quality working condition?

Buying Vintage/Used Turntables Locally

No matter where you live, there are countless sources for purchasing used and vintage turntables locally. Examples include garage sales, flea markets, thrift stores, antique shops, used audio stores, Craigslist, Kijiji (in Canada), and more. A local source is typically the best place to start, because you are able to view and test the turntable before buying.

CHECKING OUT A USED TURNTABLE

Before heading out to look at a used turntable, do some initial research on the model to familiarize yourself with it. A website called Vinyl Engine (www.vinylengine.com) has an extensive archive of manuals, schematics, and brochures for individual turntable models. Additionally, searching the model on YouTube may yield videos demonstrating how that particular turntable *should* appear and operate. This will give you a general idea of what to expect. Also, be sure to bring along a few records, just in case the seller does not have any, and request that the seller play some records so you can hear how the turntable sounds.

BUDGETING BASICS

When buying a used turntable, it is key to find out if replacement parts are needed and work the cost of those into your overall budget. You don't want to think you've scored a bargain $50 turntable only to discover that you need to buy a $350 part to make it work.

Here is a list of what you should examine:

1. **Power source:** Plug in the turntable to ensure it turns on. If there are issues with it turning on, don't buy it. Fixing that mechanism is too costly and difficult. If it turns on with no issues, run through the following observations.
2. **Platter:** Put your hand on the platter and feel if it is wobbly or creaky. On the majority of turntables, you can remove the platter to examine it. If this is possible, look for two large holes that your fingers can be inserted into to gently remove the platter. Once you have done this, observe the bottom of the platter and plinth below the platter for any signs of wear and tear. If the turntable has been used heavily for DJing, signs of damage to the platter and components on the base will be obvious, and it may be best to avoid purchasing. Finally, rotate the platter back and forth

and confirm that it can spin in both directions without dragging.

3. **Headshell:** If possible, remove the cartridge and examine for signs of heavy usage such as scratches or missing screws. If the turntable has had heavy usage and has gone through frequent stylus and cartridge changes, you will recognize obvious signs of wear and tear within the headshell.

4. **Cue lever:** Test the cue lever to assure it works. A working cue lever should drop the stylus to the record smoothly in addition to lifting it off the record softly but effortlessly.

5. **Plinth:** Observe the entire base of the turntable to assure no screws are missing. Minor scratches are okay, but assure there are no signs of the turntable ever being dropped such as large dents, deep scratches, and so on.

6. **Cables:** Examine the RCA, ground wire, and other cables to assure there are no breaks or exposed wire.

7. **Mechanics:** Now it is time to play a record!

    1. Place the record on the turntable and begin playing the record with whatever method is supplied—for a cue lever, manually move the stylus; if automatic, hit the start and stop button. Make sure things work correctly.

    2. Switch between speeds several times to make sure they are all working correctly.

    3. Test all available functions, including the pitch control and strobe lights. If you're looking at an automatic turntable, those specific functions should work flawlessly.

    4. Let the turntable run for as long as possible, up to fifteen minutes, and assure no burning smell is observed.

Online

If you are not successful in locating potential turntables locally, there are a few places online, such as eBay and Goodwill, that are excellent sources for a used turntable. Similar to eBay, Goodwill has a section where you can bid for a turntable online at: www.shopgoodwill.com. If you are considering purchasing a turntable through Goodwill or eBay, do as much research as possible on the equipment and only purchase if the price point is a great value. There are often vague details provided and no guarantees within auction websites, so that's a risk you'll take using them.

If you are in pursuit of a high-grade turntable and are willing to purchase used, consider SoundStage Direct, an online store based out of Pennsylvania. This company offers a "Certified Pre-Owned" turntable selection (in addition to a wide variety of new turntables). They offer extremely reputable and premium brands, such as VPI, Rega, Clearaudio, Thorens, Marantz, Pro-Ject Audio, and more.

SoundStage Direct acquires their Certified Pre-Owned turntables through a trade-in program, where you can trade in your current turntable for credit toward a new turntable purchase. Once they receive the used turntable, a trained technician examines it prior to resale. SoundStage Direct offers a warranty between thirty and ninety days, depending on the turntable purchased. Details of available turntables can be viewed on their website, but call them with questions about the specific turntable you are purchasing. Certified Pre-Owned and other discounted turntables are available here: www.soundstagedirect.com/open-box.shtml.

Specific Recommended Used/Vintage Turntable Models

If you decide to purchase a used turntable, you'll need to be ready to replace the cartridge and stylus. For that reason, I've included a few highly recommended stylus/cartridge pairings.

MARANTZ 6110

The Marantz 6110 turntable was the first turntable I owned. I purchased it used for $150 and equipped it with a brand-new Audio-Technica ATN70 cartridge. Vintage Marantz receivers are also highly recommended. Pairing a used Marantz turntable and a high-quality receiver can create a unique, warm sound.

Basic Specs
- Typical price range: $75–$300
- Two speed settings: 33⅓ and 45 rpm
- Belt drive
- Manual turntable

Advantages
- Often readily available for a low cost
- Replacement parts are affordable

Disadvantages
- On occasion, requires quite a bit of tinkering to achieve optimal audio
- RCA cable is not detachable

Stylus/Cartridge Replacement Options
- Audio-Technica ATN70 ($49)

REGA PLANAR 3

Although the Rega Planar 3 turntable is available new to-day (at around $1,000), the Rega 3 is a classic audiophile turntable that has been manufactured since the 1970s. The Rega 3 has been through four principle model names: Planar 3 (1977–2000), P3 (2000–2007), P3-24 (2007–2012), and RP3 (2013–present). Unlike other turntables, the Rega is light-weight to control unwanted resonance and vibrations that produce feedback. Few other turntables have maintained the reputable high-fidelity status than the Rega.

Basic Specs
- Typical price range: $100–$450
- Two speed settings: 33⅓ and 45 rpm
- Belt drive
- Manual turntable
- Glass platter

Advantages
- Constructed with lightweight materials in order to provide quality sound output
- Minimalistic turntable that requires little to no tweaking by users
- Has been highly regarded as an audiophile turntable since the 1970s
- If needed, replacement parts are readily available and fairly priced

Disadvantages
- Due to their popularity, may be difficult to find

Stylus/Cartridge Replacement Options

- Rega Bias 2 ($165)
- Denon DL-110 ($249)

TECHNICS SL-1200

Panasonic (formerly Matsushita) manufactured the Technics SL-1200 from 1972 until 2010. The turntable was released as a high-fidelity turntable and was popular among both club and radio DJs. It is widely regarded for its durability and being an overall reliable turntable.

Basic Specs

- Typical price range: $50–$1,200
- Two speed settings: 33⅓ and 45 rpm
- Direct drive
- Manual turntable
- Includes pitch adjustment

Advantages

- Constructed using high-quality materials, with the bulk of the parts made from metal
- Direct drive with high-torque design, meaning the platter will promptly spin at the desired speed
- Extremely reliable and has proven to last decades with heavy use

Disadvantages

- Due to their popularity, they are at times extremely difficult to locate
- They tend to be on the higher side of the price range due to their popularity

- These turntables were heavily used for club and radio DJing, so thoroughly inspect for wear and tear

BUYER BEWARE

When checking out a Technics SL-1200, bear in mind that this turntable may have been used for DJing. Inspect the turntable closely to find out if included parts are replacement parts. There are a number of exceptionally detailed videos on YouTube that will allow you to become familiar with how these turntables appear and function.

Stylus/Cartridge Replacement Options
- Shure M97xE ($99)
- Audio-Technica AT440MLa ($209)

THORENS TD-124/TD-124 MK2
The TD-124 was a turntable manufactured by Thorens between 1957 and 1968 that offered a host of features never before seen in other turntables. Although these are more expensive than other used turntables, this model will give you a true vintage audiophile experience.

Basic Specs
- Typical price range: $1,000 +
- Iron-cast platter that weighs approximately 9.4 pounds
- Four speed settings: 33⅓, 45, 78, and the rarely found 16⅔ rpm
- Belt drive and idler-wheel drive

Advantages
- A phenomenal turntable! Produces rich and coherent sound
- Has the ability to play four speeds

Disadvantages
- Can be pricey
- Replacement parts can be expensive and difficult to find

Purchasing a New Turntable

Similar to buying a new car, it is essential to understand all the possible features and benefits to determine which ones are right for you. Be sure to try the turntables that interest you.

When purchasing a new turntable, here are some key points to consider:

- What is your overall budget (and include having to potentially buy speakers and a receiver!)?
- Where will you place your turntable (be sure you know your size and weight limitations)?
- Do you want an automatic or manual turntable?
- Do you want a turntable with a built-in preamp?
- Do you need a USB option?

Under $150

Yes, you can buy a complete turntable setup for under $150. Less than a $100, actually! All-in-one turntables are true plug-and-play setups—you don't have to buy separate preamps, receivers, and speakers. You simply remove your turntable from the box, plug it in, put on a record, and you are ready to enjoy your music.

However, there are a few drawbacks to these portable, inexpensive systems:

- The speakers on these systems are limited and can produce a muffled sound. They are often less audible than speakers on a cell phone.
- These turntables don't include a counterweight or antiskate control, which can cause your stylus to skip through the grooves and not play through records correctly.
- The stylus and cartridge included are cheap, plastic, and not upgradable. Additionally, there are a multitude of complaints regarding how the styluses on these turntables can damage your record collection.

Those drawbacks aside, these all-in-one turntables are perfect for portable and infrequent use. Say you are hosting a BBQ and want to play records outside. Or you want to be able to spin records while camping in the woods for a week. Having a portable turntable handy is a tremendous way to easily play music away from your permanent setup.

RECORD RUNNER VW RECORD PLAYER

Originally known as the Soundwagon, the Record Runner is the world's smallest portable vinyl record player—it can actually fit in the palm of your hand. This turntable is essentially a miniature toy Volkswagen car. You place the Volkswagen car onto a record and it "drives" around the grooves of the album, playing the music.

Another benefit of an all-in-one system is for children who are interested in exploring and playing with records. Consider it a step up from the classic Fisher-Price turntable, which has a discography limited to a few nursery rhymes. Young children are not likely to properly handle and clean their records—so instead, let them play around with a simple, low-budget turntable! Here are a few options under $100:

- Jensen JTA-222 3-Speed Turntable ($40)
- Jensen JTA-230 ($49)
- Crosley Cruiser Portable 3-Speed Turntable ($79)

Following are a few options under $150 that are decent for a beginner's setup.

AUDIO-TECHNICA AT-LP60 WITH USB

The Audio-Technica AT-LP60 is a great beginner's turntable within the lower price range. It is a fully automatic turntable that includes a preamp, allowing you to easily connect it to an existing receiver and speaker setup or plug your headphones right into it. The USB model includes a USB output, allowing you to connect it to your computer as an output source or to record and convert the audio to a digital format.

Basic Specs
- Price: $99; with USB: $129
- Fully automatic
- Built-in preamp
- Two speed settings: 33⅓ and 45 rpm
- Belt drive
- Integral Dual Magnet phono cartridge with replaceable diamond stylus
- Die-cast aluminum platter

- USB model includes a USB port, allowing you to connect to your computer
- Wow/flutter: 0.25%

Advantages
- Reasonably priced beginner's fully automatic turntable
- Preamp included, but it can be bypassed
- Includes a magnetic cartridge, which is better than ceramic cartridges
- Audio-Technica has a reputation for producing high-quality products

Disadvantages
- Cartridge is not upgradable; only the stylus is
- Occasional complaints include minor speed variances and noticeable flutter and wows

NUMARK TTUSB
If you are relying on using USB as an output for the audio or want to convert audio digitally, the Numark is a suitable turntable for this.

Basic Specs
- Price: $139
- Manual
- Built-in preamp
- Two speed settings: 33⅓ and 45 rpm
- Belt drive
- Adjustable antiskate control
- Pitch control
- USB connectivity
- Preamp not required

- Wow/flutter: not listed

Advantages
- Cartridge is replaceable
- Adjustable pitch control (+/- 10%)

Disadvantages
- Dust cover not included; you'd have to purchase separately
- Does not include a cueing lever or automatic stop/start
- If you are not planning to utilize the USB feature, the sound quality of this turntable is inferior to the Audio-Technica AT-LP60 and Pioneer PL-990
- Built-in preamp cannot be bypassed

PIONEER PL-990

The Pioneeer PL-990 is an entry-level, fully automatic turntable that has received positive reviews for its sound quality within its price range. It is designed similarly to the classic black turntables of the 1960s and 1970s and has an added retro design.

Basic Specs
- Price: $135
- Fully automatic
- Built-in preamp
- Two speed settings: 33⅓ and 45 rpm
- Belt drive
- Moving-magnet cartridge
- Pitch control with a strobe light
- Aluminum platter

THE BEGINNER'S GUIDE TO VINYL

- Wow/flutter: 0.25%

Advantages
- Reasonably priced beginner's turntable
- Includes a built-in preamp
- Includes a magnetic cartridge, which is preferred over ceramic cartridges

Disadvantages
- Cartridge is not replaceable
- Constructed of plastic materials; feels flimsy
- The RCA cable included is fairly short
- No preamp bypass; you cannot connect into a phono source

$150–$300

Within the $150–$300 range, you are able to purchase good-quality turntables that have more features and flexibility. Both Pro-Ject Audio and Music Hall, higher-end turntable manufacturers, offer entry-level turntables in this range that live up to their value.

AUDIO-TECHNICA AT-LP60-BT
Audio-Technica now offers the LP60 in a BT model ($179), which includes the ability to connect your turntable to speakers via Bluetooth. For the full features and specs, check out the Audio-Technica AT-LP60 in the previous section—it's the same as this model minus the Bluetooth feature.

AUDIO-TECHNICA AT-LP120-USB

This turntable is highly recommended for both casual everyday use and for those who are interested in learning to DJ. It is easy to use, so it's perfect for a family setup. The design mimics the Technics SL-1200, and includes features usually found on big-ticket turntables, such as pitch control, strobe light, and the ability to balance the tone arm. The Audio-Technica LP120-USB offers you an affordable way to listen to records without a complicated setup.

This is the second turntable I own. It is regularly used in our retail stores for spinning records and demonstrating records for customers. We also, on occasion, even use this turntable as a secondary turntable when listening to and approving test pressings.

Basic Specs
- Price: $299
- Manual with cueing lever
- Built-in preamp
- Three speed settings: 33⅓, 45, and 78 rpm
- Direct-drive, high-torque motor
- Pitch control with strobe lights
- USB connectivity
- Cast aluminum platter with included slip mat
- Wow/flutter: 0.20%

Advantages
- Has the ability to play three speeds; however, if you intend on playing 78-rpm records, you'll need to acquire a stylus specifically for this purpose
- Ability to play records forward and reverse
- Adjustable pitch control with strobe lights

- Built-in preamp is switchable, meaning you can use it and avoid buying a preamp or you can bypass it and use another preamp source
- The cartridge included is decent but can also be upgraded
- Due to its popularity within the market, you might be able to find it on sale for less than the MSRP of $299

Disadvantages
- Primarily constructed of plastic
- RCA cables are not detachable and if ever need to be replaced, it'd be a hassle
- If you want to bypass the preamp, a ground wire is not included; a hum is produced and you believe it is caused by the lack of a ground wire, you can add one manually

MUSIC HALL MMF USB-1

The MMF USB-1 is Music Hall's entry-level turntable. It is a convenient and practical turntable that includes a USB option, allowing you to digitize your records. It includes a built-in phono preamp, cartridge, dust cover, and all other components to allow you to just plug in and play.

Basic Specs
- Price: $249
- Manual with cueing lever
- Built-in preamp
- Two speed settings: 33⅓ and 45 rpm
- Belt drive
- Pitch control
- Antiskating

- Audio-Technica AT3600L magnetic cartridge supplied
- USB connectivity
- Aluminum die-cast platter
- Wow/flutter: 0.25%

Advantages
- Includes an S-shaped tone arm with a premounted Audio-Technica AT3600L phono cartridge
- Includes pitch control and strobe lighting
- Built-in preamp, which can be bypassed
- The cartridge included is decent but can be upgraded

Disadvantages
- Has a higher wow/flutter percentage in comparison to other turntables within this price range
- Does not include the dual plinth that other, higher-end Music Hall turntables have

PRO-JECT ESSENTIAL II

This turntable is for the true audiophile on a budget. Pro-Ject is a reputable manufacturer of high-end audiophile equipment. With their entry-level turntable, the Essential II, Pro-Ject implemented a simple design allowing them to focus on a high-quality output at an extremely reasonable price point.

Basic Specs
- Price: $299
- Manual with tone arm lift lever
- Two speed settings: 33⅓ and 45 rpm (speeds are changed manually)
- Belt drive with a silicone belt

- Ortofon OM 5E cartridge
- No built-in preamp
- Antiskating weight adjustment scale
- Wow/flutter: 0.12%

Advantages
- Includes a premounted Ortofon OM 5E cartridge, a magnetic cartridge highly regarded by audiophiles
- Quiet and smooth-running motor with silicone belt
- Solid, sturdy plinth, but is still fairly lightweight (8.8 pounds)
- This is an impeccable turntable for the audiophile on a budget, as it produces a sophisticated sound quality

Disadvantages
- Requires some initial, but not generally problematic, setup due to the way the belt is placed on the platter and can be a bit difficult to get right during initial assembly

$300–$500

In the $300–$500 price range, you start finding higher-quality components, such as better cartridges, tone arms, and overall build materials.

MUSIC HALL MMF-2.3
The Music Hall MMF-2.3 is a two-speed, belt-driven audiophile turntable at a fairly reasonable price. It's built with high-quality components typically found in Music Hall products, such as high-precision stainless steel and bronze bear-

ings, gold RCA connectors, an alloy platter, and vibration-dampening adjustable feet.

Basic Specs
- Price: $499
- Manual
- Two speed settings: 33⅓ and 45 rpm
- Belt drive
- Includes a Music Hall Spirit moving-magnet cartridge and elliptical-shaped stylus, which increases the ability of the stylus to accurately follow the groove
- Top-tier 8.6-inch carbon fiber tone arm
- Aluminum headshell
- Alloy platter and felt mat
- Wow/flutter: 0.10%

Advantages
- Fairly quick and easy to assemble—premounted cartridge and tone arm make it virtually ready to plug and play
- High-quality construction, including a heavy steel alloy platter, vibration-dampening feet, carbon tone arm, and a Music Hall Spirit cartridge with an elliptical stylus

Disadvantages
- Does not include the dual-plinth construction found in their higher-priced turntables

PRO-JECT DEBUT CARBON
A step up from the previously mentioned Pro-Ject Essential II, this turntable provides you with several upgrades: a preinstalled (and highly regarded) Ortofon 2M Red cartridge,

a metal platter (as opposed to the MDF platter on the Essential II), and an overall improved, quality build.

Basic Specs
- Price: $449
- Manual
- Two speed settings: 33⅓ and 45 rpm
- Belt drive
- Metal platter with felt mat
- Carbon tone arm
- Ortofon 2M Red cartridge
- Wow/Flutter: 0.10%
- Built-in preamp

Advantages
- Includes a carbon tube tone arm, which increases stiffness and decreases resonance, and is not usually found within this price point
- Includes a highly regarded Ortofon 2M Red cartridge (retails for $99 separately)
- Extremely lightweight turntable that can be moved and transported with ease
- Available in various colors: purple, green, blue, yellow, black, silver, and white

Disadvantages
- Requires the purchase of a preamp or receiver with built-in preamp; however, you can purchase the Pro-Ject Debut Carbon Phono USB ($549), which includes a built-in preamp in addition to all the other features mentioned here

REGA RP1

The RP1 is Rega's entry-level turntable, and it features high-quality components and outstanding performance within its price point.

Basic Specs
- Price: $445
- Manual
- Two speed settings: 33⅓ and 45 rpm
- Belt drive
- Rega carbon moving-magnet cartridge
- Rega RB101 tone arm
- Phenolic resin platter
- Wow/flutter: not provided by manufacturer

Advantages
- Rega boasts that this simplistically designed turntable is "plug and play" ready with a setup time less than 30 seconds
- Boasts a high-quality, low-vibration motor
- Includes the hand-assembled, highly regarded RB101 tone arm
- Can be further upgraded with the purchase of a $195 Performance Pack, which includes an upgraded drive belt, the Rega Bias 2 cartridge, and a turntable mat, plus Rega will automatically balance and set the tracking weight for the Rega Bias 2

Disadvantages
- For this price point, it is challenging to identify unjustifiable disadvantages; one minor consideration is that you have to change the speed manually

$500–$1,000

Moving up into this price range will provide you with a significant step up in audio performance. You will be able to acquire a turntable that will provide you with phenomenal sound for considerable years to come. If you value quality sound, but are not yet willing to invest thousands upon thousands, this is an excellent starting point.

MUSIC HALL MMF-5.3

This is the third turntable I own, which I spin records on on a regular basis. Our label, SRCVinyl, utilizes this turntable for both reviewing and approving test pressings in addition to casual listening. I have had the turntable for approximately a year and am still using the Music Hall Magic 3 magnet cartridge, which was specifically built for Music Hall by Ortofon. I intended to eventually upgrade the cartridge, but have not yet done so because the Music Hall Magic 3 still sounds phenomenal. My Music Hall is paired with a Yamaha A-S500 receiver (with a built-in preamp), Totem Mite speakers, and AKG K240 MKII headphones.

Basic Specs
- Price: $875
- Manual turntable
- Two speed settings: 33⅓ and 45 rpm
- Belt drive
- Includes a Music Hall Magic 3 cartridge with the MMF-5.1 model and the Ortofon 2M Blue cartridge with the MMF-5.3 Model
- Wow/flutter: 0.15%

Advantages

- The cartridge and stylus included are a $350 value. The cartridge comes properly mounted and aligned.
- The base is built with two plinths with dampening in between the platforms. The top platform holds the main bearing, platter, tone arm, and cartridge, while the bottom platform holds the motor, switch, wiring, and feet. This is constructed this way to allow the turntable to isolate vibrations.
- You can upgrade components such as cartridge, stylus, platter, and legs.
- You can fine-tune by adjusting counterweight and antiskating.

Disadvantages

- Speeds need to be changed manually, but it is an uncomplicated process.
- Unlike the VPI (see this price range section), it is not plug and play, and set up may be a bit complicated for novice turntable users. However, if you buy one through a quality local electronics dealer, they should be able to assist you if you run into issues.
- Requires a preamp or receiver with built-in preamp.

PRO-JECT 1 XPRESSION CARBON

The 1 Xpression Carbon model has been manufactured by Pro-Ject since 1991. The current version includes a heavy steel platter, a new carbon tone arm, and an Ortofon 2M Red cartridge.

Basic Specs
- Price: $999
- Manual turntable
- Belt drive
- Two speed settings: 33⅓ and 45 rpm
- Heavy steel sandwich platter with rubber dampening below for superior resonance (deep and full sound)
- Ortofon 2M Red cartridge
- 8.6-inch carbon tone arm

Advantages
- Upgrades and differences from the Pro-Ject Debut Carbon model include a heavy steel platter with rubber dampening and upgraded coned feet, motor, power supply, tone arm, and cartridge.
- Turntable components are built with quality materials (gold-plated RCA cables, heavy steel sandwich platter, carbon tone arm), which is reflected by the high sound quality it produces.

Disadvantages
- Setup is relatively manageable but may be a bit difficult for turntable novices. However, if you buy this at a quality local electronics dealer, they should be able to assist you if you run into issues.
- Requires a preamp or receiver with built-in preamp.

VPI NOMAD
VPI Industries is based in New Jersey and has been manufacturing state-of-the-art turntables since 1978. The Nomad is VPI's entry-level turntable (their other models head upward in price to as high as over $20,000!). This turntable is highly regarded as a truly high-performance turntable.

Basic Specs

- Price: $999
- Manual
- Two speed settings: 33⅓ and 45 rpm
- Belt drive
- Includes Ortofon 2M Red cartridge
- 10-inch gimbaled/yoke-bearing tone arm
- Built-in preamp and headphone amplifier
- Wow/flutter: 0.06%

Advantages

- Unlike numerous pricey high-end turntables, the tone arm and cartridge are included: Ortofon 2M Red cartridge ($99) and 10-inch gimbaled/yoke-bearing tone arm
- Straightforward assembly—remove from the box, put the platter over the spindle, plug in, and you are ready to begin spinning records!
- Headphone amplifier is a beneficial addition for those who like to listen to records with headphones

Disadvantages

- Built-in phonostage cannot be bypassed, and you cannot use an outboard phono preamp

$1,000 +

A single record groove is tinier than the width of a human hair, which means the precision of a turntable is of utmost importance. If you decide to invest thousands of dollars in a turntable, much of what you're paying for is increased fidelity and precision. Components of these turntables, such as tone arms, cartridges, and platters, plus speakers and receivers, are built with one goal: to produce as much accuracy and precision possible to reproduce the sound to its utmost capacity.

For a truly impressive setup, you can easily invest tens of thousands of dollars on a turntable alone, in addition to adding premium components such as preamps, tone arms, cartridges, platters, speakers, receivers, and so on. Instead of listing individual turntables, I have summarized various high-end manufacturers that sell turntables for more than $1,000 and the different models they offer.

CLEARAUDIO

Based in Germany, Clearaudio Electronic GmbH is recognizable by its transparent turntable models. Clearaudio meticulously creates everything by hand and offers guaranteed absence of resonance when playing records. Their entry-level turntable, dubbed the Concept, bears a $1,400 sticker price (before a cartridge is even added!), but is essentially a plug-and-play system that boasts a crisp sound, with even finicky records. It is all upward in price from there, with several turntables under the $5,000 mark . . . but a few over the $100,000 mark! Here are the current Clearaudio models and their approximate price points:

- Concept: $1,400–$2,999
- Emotion SE: $2,500
- Performance DC: $3,000–$5,500
- Ovation: $6,500–$10,000
- Innovation Compact: $10,000–$12,000
- Innovation: $13,500–$15,000
- Master Innovation: $30,000
- Statement: $170,000

MCINTOSH

McIntosh has been manufacturing audiophile turntables for decades and currently offers two models—the McIntosh MT5, which will run you $6,500, and the McIntosh MT10, which costs approximately $8,000. Both McIntosh models boast moving-coil cartridges and a solid silicone and acrylic platter weighing 5 pounds that measures 1½ inches thick that floats with magnetic force as opposed to the use of ball bearings at the base. The features on this turntable are endless and are aesthetically complemented by the classic McIntosh green glowing platter, matching its light-up front glass panel. McIntosh products cannot be purchased online—you can only buy them through an authorized dealer (which you can locate on their website). I highly recommend that every vinyl enthusiast finds an opportunity to experience a McIntosh turntable at least once in a lifetime.

REGA

I have mentioned Rega a few times now because everything they produce is of notable quality and worth the amount spent. Rega was founded in the UK in 1973 and manufactures not only turntables but cartridges, tone arms, and award-winning amplifiers and speakers.

WOODEN TURNTABLES

Audiowood manufactures wooden turntables, speakers, and other AV equipment. They currently hand-produce the Barky turntable out of wood and high-quality Rega parts, such as a glass platter, the RB303 tone arm, and the Rega Elys 2 cartridge.

At the over $1,000 price point they offer three turntables: the RP6, at $1,495–$2,220; the RP8, at $2,995–$4,195, depending on the cartridge you select; and the RP10, at $5,495–$6,695.

VPI

VPI Industries is a family-run company cofounded by Sheila and Harry Weisfeld. Harry, a dedicated audiophile, set out to find a way to assure his records were as clean as possible. This lead to the creation of VPI's first major product, the HW-16, a record-cleaning machine still in production today (and discussed later in this book). Eventually VPI created a turntable and have continued doing so for more than thirty years. VPI turntables have always been within the higher price range, but they are highly regarded by audiophiles as worth every penny. They adamantly focus on enhancing their turntables' speed stability with their machines boasting unquestionably low wow and flutter percentages. Each turntable is individually quality controlled within their facility in New Jersey. Currently the following turntable models are available:

- Nomad: $999
- Traveler: $1,499
- Scout Jr: $1,599
- Scout: $2,199–$2,600
- Classic: $2,799–$30,000
- Classic Signature: $5,999–$6,500
- Prime: $3,999–$5,999
- Aries: $6,000
- Avenger: $9,499–$20,999
- HR-X: $12,000

Laser Turntables

A laser turntable is a turntable that uses an optical laser as opposed to a stylus. The first working laser turntable prototype, named LASERPHONE, was patented in 1976 by William K. Heine, with the hope of using lasers within record players. It wasn't until 1986 that the first prototype for a model intended for commercial release was introduced— the Finial LT-1. Benefits of the laser turntable included elimination of wear and tear on the album, tracking noise, and feedback. However, because lasers are insanely accurate, they tend to pick up every particle of dust and dirt on the record. The sale price of the Finial LT-1 was $2,500.

At the time the Finial LT-1 was created, the economy was also experiencing a major economic recession. Additionally, compact discs were becoming quite popular and affordable. This was during the time that vinyl record sales plummeted, and a multitude of turntable manufacturers went out of business.

In 1989, Finial's patents were sold to the Japanese turntable manufacturer BSR, which in turn became ELP Japan. They continued the development of the laser turntable. The first commercial laser turntable became available in 1998, with a ticket price of $20,500. The ELP LT-1XA Laser Turntable is still available with an approximate price tag of $15,000.

Setting Up Your Turntable

Once you buy your turntable and accompanying equipment, you will need to assemble it. Although exact directions may vary depending on the turntable you purchase, this section outlines basic information to support you in setting up your turntable, preamp, receiver, and speakers.

Set Up the Receiver and Speakers

Sometimes it's a good idea to set up your speakers and receiver first, since it is a fairly simple task to complete.

1. Place your receiver and speakers where you want them.
2. Connect your speakers and receiver by running the speaker wires to the receiver. Locate the speaker terminals (red and black) and place the appropriate wire inside. Some receiver terminals include clips that require you push down to place the wire, while others consist of a cap to unscrew, stick the wire in, and screw it back on again.
3. If your setup includes a separate preamp, find the corresponding connector on the receiver and connect the preamp to it.
4. Assure all components that require being plugged into an outlet are plugged in at this point (typically your receiver and preamp need to be plugged into an outlet).
5. If there is an uncomplicated way to test that the speakers and receiver are working correctly, such as plugging in an iPod, do so now. This way you can assure the speakers and receiver are connected properly before setting up the turntable.

SPEAKER WIRE CARE
Make sure you have some slack in your speaker wires so they don't pull the equipment or become damaged. Also, label your speaker wires where you connect them into the receiver so if you ever have to disconnect your receiver, you'll be able to quickly identify where they go when it's time to hook them up again.

Turntable

Each turntable will include unique, specific requirements for how it is assembled. Refer to your manual during setup and keep the following tips in mind.

Typical steps to assembling a turntable:

1. Remove the turntable and all its components from the box.
2. Place the turntable on the spot you have selected for it. Find a sturdy place for it to sit since that arrangement will provide the best performance output.
3. If your turntable has adjustable feet, be sure to adjust them so that your turntable sits flat.
4. Follow the manual to complete all assembly tasks. Most turntables under $1,000 should not require a great deal of assembly. Possible assembly tasks may include placing the platter onto its spot on the plinth, installing the cartridge, installing the dust cover, and attaching it to your receiver.
5. You may be required to adjust the tracking force (more on that next).

YES, YOU DO HAVE TO READ THE MANUAL
Read through the manual and all steps *thoroughly* before starting!!! Over the years, I have become a master at assembling various items, from trampolines to kitchen cabinets, and I attribute it all to one factor: I read through the entire directions from beginning to end before I start. As I assemble, prior to starting one step I reread that step along with the following step, providing me with a clear idea of what I am doing. The majority of turntables are not troublesome to assemble, if assembly is even required.

ADJUSTING THE TRACKING FORCE

Adjusting the tracking force, often referred to as balancing the tone arm, is the most significant adjustment you will make to optimize the output from your new turntable. The manual provided with your turntable will explain how to tackle this if it is required. Following is a basic tone arm–balancing method, but consult a professional if you have any doubts.

1. Install your cartridge and place a record on the platter.
2. Set the antiskate setting to 0.
3. Transfer the tone arm over the platter about 1 inch inward from the edge of the platter. While still holding the tone arm off the platter, begin turning the counterweight in either direction, whichever allows it to balance in a way that allows the arm to float on its own. When properly floating it will be completely even and parallel with the platter.
4. Once it is balanced, slowly turn the counterweight and set it to 0. The tone arm is now calibrated.
5. Set the counterweight dial to indicate the desired weight given by the manufacturer.
6. Adjust the antiskate dial to approximately the same number.

TRACKING FORCE GAUGE

A tracking force gauge is essentially a scale for your tone arm that provides you with an accurately balanced tone arm. A tracking force gauge can be purchased for as little as $30–$50 and is often included with higher-end turntables. To operate a tracking force gauge, you place the gauge on your platter, then place the stylus onto the designated spot on the gauge. The gauge will show you the exact weight the stylus applies.

Be extremely patient while adjusting the tracking force. The more you slow down and don't rush the process, the easier this will be.

> **TOOLKIT TIP**
> Using a level to assure that your turntable is completely flat will ensure that your setup has a good foundation for playing records properly.

A Few Don'ts for Caring for Your Turntable

Now you should be ready to begin playing records! Before you head out to buy records (if you haven't already acquired a stack or two), let's review basic information for caring for your brand-new turntable.

Never Play a Wet Record!

Sometimes DJs spray a mist on records before playing them. The water spray is meant to act as a lubricant that quiets crackles and pops. Doing this will not only cause dirty records to become dirtier, but it also can damage your stylus and cartridge and possibly other turntable components.

Don't Touch a Spinning Platter

Never touch a record or platter while it is spinning. This can scratch both the platter and the record.

Don't Touch the Grooves

Avoid touching the record in the area with the grooves with your hands at all times. You can handle them by placing your hand and fingers on the sides, similar to how you handle a CD, or you can touch the center label. Some audiophiles recommend wearing white gloves, but this isn't necessary because if you do accidently touch the record, it can easily be cleaned before playing.

Don't Use Lighter Fluid!

A turntable stylus reacts to vibrations and picking up dust or dirt can interfere with how a record plays (in addition to damaging your equipment). Clearly, you need to keep your turntable clean. However, follow the manufacturer's cleaning directions for the turntable, cartridge, and stylus. Be wary of advice online that encourages you to use obscure household items to clean your turntable!

DO I SPIN RECORDS WITH THE DUST COVER UP OR DOWN?
Some people suggest that if you have animals or even the tiniest accumulation of dust and dirt within your home that you should play your records with the dust cover closed. However, others argue that closing the dust cover while playing your records can negatively affect the audio. I side with the latter—your records and turntable will always collect dust, and I'd rather not risk compromising the sound quality so I keep the dust cover open while spinning a record.

Don't Forget about the Ground Wire

In the beginning of this chapter we discussed the ground wire, a skinny wire that plugs into a screw or post (often marked "ground") on the preamp or receiver. This wire is used to prevent a ground loop that diverts feedback, in turn creating an audible humming noise. However, sometimes the opposite problem happens. If you hear an audible hum, try adding or removing the ground wire to see if that solves the problem.

Cleaning the Stylus

No matter how clean your records are, the stylus will always attract dust. Dust should always be removed from a stylus before playing a record. This prevents degradation of the stylus, lengthens the lifespan of your records, and improves the sound quality of your records. The manufacturer of your stylus provides you with an hours of use rating, specific to your stylus, which typically is between 2,000 and 3,000 hours. Cleaning your stylus when dirty ensures you reach the highest amount of playing hours possible.

There are several stylus-cleaning brushes and fluids designed specifically to assist with the cleaning of the stylus. There are various stylus cleaners available; these models are highly preferred by audiophiles:

- Last Stylus Cleaner 4 ($25)
- The Disc Doctor's Stylus Cleaner ($28)
- Clearaudio Diamond Elixir Stylus Cleaner ($30)
- Onzow Zerodust ($69)

Although many retailers carry these stylus cleaners in addition to others, visit Jerry Raskin's Needle Doctor website (www.needledoctor.com) before purchasing any, because they specialize in the sale of cartridges and styluses. The Needle Doctor website includes a lot of specific information for each brand, including instructions on how the cleaner is to be used.

Replacing Your Cartridge/Stylus

The cartridge and stylus are both rated for a certain amount of playback hours and at some point will need to be replaced. Upgrading to a higher-quality cartridge and stylus can be an easy way to boost your system's sound quality. A reputable retailer will be able to tell you not only which stylus and cartridge are compatible with your equipment, but can provide guidance on how to install it.

Cartridge

There is an abundance of choices when it comes to choosing to replace or update your cartridge, and there will always be a debate as to which is superior.

- Moving magnets are simple to use and the least expensive.
- Moving iron track with less pressure and are viewed by some to have less tracking issues.
- Moving-coil cartridges are higher in cost, frequently require amplification in addition to your preamp, but are viewed as sonically superior.

Cartridges are infrequently replaced due to damage but can be replaced as an upgrade or if a compatible stylus is no longer available. If you decide to replace your cartridge, refer to the manual for directions on how to install that specific model.

Stylus

Styluses are more likely to be replaced than cartridges. Luckily, they are fairly inexpensive and rather effortless to change out. Follow manufacturer's instructions to replace them.

CHAPTER 5

Vinyl Collectors' Terminology

*a*s you start to build your vinyl collection, you'll find a whole new language of terms and lingo that you'll need to understand and use in your transactions. No matter what type of vinyl you pick up or where, there are basic terms avid vinyl collectors use. Familiarize yourself with these terms, and you'll be able to converse with buyers with ease and confidence.

The Plural of Vinyl Is Not Vinyls . . . or Is It?

One way to be easily identified as a record-buying newbie is to say the word "vinyls." Record-collecting aficionados insist that you never say *vinyls*. Instead, when referring to multiple records, call them vinyl or vinyl records. However, in 2012, Mark Liberman, professor of linguistics at the University of Pennsylvania, argued on his blog, *Language Log*, that this is essentially an invented rule and that *vinyls* is an acceptable term. Regardless of what side of the debate you land on, be on the safe side and avoid saying *vinyls* when shopping.

Audiophile

Although the term "audiophile" can refer to a type of collector, a specific record pressing can also be referred to as an audiophile pressing. Although there is no official standard of exactly what an audiophile pressing is, the generally accepted definition is a record that is heavy in weight, mastered with the best available sources, and manufactured using quality techniques and careful procedures.

Here are a few indicators if a release labeled audiophile truly is an audiophile pressing:

- Pressed on black virgin vinyl. Colored vinyl doesn't always have the same sound quality as black vinyl.
- Detailed mastering information is provided, such as the exact source used and the engineer or studio who mastered it.

- Pressed on heavyweight 180- to 200-gram vinyl. Although I do not believe this enhances the sound quality, it does help avoid warping.
- Made with quality audio sources, not sourced from commercial CDs or low-quality digital audio.

Leaders in Audiophile Pressings

Mobile Fidelity Sound Lab (MoFi) is credited as the leader and pioneer of audiophile recordings and has been releasing audiophile records since 1977. Mobile Fidelity's line of high-end vinyl, dubbed Original Master Recording, introduced "half-speed" mastering, meaning the lacquers are cut at 16⅔ rpm, half the normal playing speed. The albums are mastered this way to ensure a precise and complete transfer of the original musical source.

One mastering engineer in particular, Stan Ricker, is closely associated with half-speed mastering and is responsible for a considerable number of the early Mobile Fidelity half-speed-mastered releases. Stan mastered and cut all his vinyl releases using this method, which can be recognized by his signature SR/2 carved within the matrix, which is an alphanumeric code stamped or handwritten on the dead wax area of a record. The majority of the vinyl titles released through our label, SRCVinyl, were half-speed mastered by Stan Ricker. He cut projects for us just days before he passed away in July of 2015. With his passing not only was a legend lost, but also potentially a quality audio mastering technique—he had no known protégé, and only a few are still practicing this method.

There are several other quality mastering techniques that are used for audiophile pressings.

Remastered

Large portions of album reissues are often marketed with stickers indicating that they are "remastered." This simply means that the original recording is remastered and may sound different than previous pressings. Remastering can be a positive attribute of a release, provided a worthy engineer is used and the original source that he masters from is of quality. Within the "remastered" category you might see variations, such as "mastered from original source" or "direct metal mastering."

Mastered from the Original Source

This term means that the music source used is the original recorded source. As an example, say an album was originally released in the 1980s and the master was originally recorded and stored onto a tape. If the album continued being successful, there may be additional master copies that were made, especially digital copies that were created in the digital era. Periodically, record labels will also duplicate from a commercial CD or a low-quality digital file, the same as anyone can purchase anywhere, as their source to save the additional money it costs to acquire the original master.

The original master is usually the highest-quality master available. Therefore, if an album is advertised as "mastered from the original source," you are likely obtaining a high-caliber record as opposed to ones pressed from CD sources.

Direct Metal Mastering (DMM)

This is the practice of cutting the album audio directly into a metal copper disc as opposed to the lacquer-coated aluminum disc typically used. Many audiophiles believe that this method is sonically superior. This process not only removes various stages of plating when manufacturing, but it also improves noise reduction and pre-echoes, which are faint but audible sounds on an album that you hear slightly before the main recording. Although this technique was once quite popular, it's now scarce because Neumann, the original manufacturer of these lathes, sold the company to Sennheiser and modern lathes and supplies are no longer produced. The lathes that are used today are independently kept and only the engineers who own them know how to use them. There are a few record manufacturers throughout Europe that have DMM facilities. However, it appears as if the art of DMM is no longer present in the United States, as the last company sold its equipment in an auction to the Church of Scientology several years ago. Rumor has it that the Church of Scientology bought up several DMM machines, which they utilize to record, transcribe, and archive L. Ron Hubbard's speeches.

Matrix Area/Dead Wax

This is the area on a record between the center label and where the grooves end. To aid in identifying the plates used to press the record and the records themselves, if a generic, white center label is used, an alphanumeric code is etched into this dead wax area.

Record Weight

Typically measured in grams, this is the weight of vinyl used to create the record. The standard weight for newly pressed 12-inch LPs is typically between 120 and 150 grams. Records that are more than 150 grams of vinyl are considered "heavyweight" and of higher quality. These typically weigh in at 180 and 200 grams.

The groove that is carved into the record does not significantly change based on the volume of vinyl used to create the record. Having said that, heavier-weighted vinyl tends to warp less and provides a stable platform for your stylus.

Etching

This is an image that is etched onto an unplayable side of your record. It does not contain audio grooves or music, but instead adds an aesthetically pleasing facet to the record. An etching is commonly made onto single 12-inch EPs that have music on only one side or on double LPs that contain music on three out of four sides.

Jacket Types

You'll encounter several different types of vinyl jackets as you build your collection. Here are some common variations.

Single Jacket

This is your standard LP jacket that usually holds a single LP. The spine on these jackets can be widened, typically called a wide spine jacket, allowing two LPs to fit inside.

Gatefold Jacket

The gatefold jacket is a type of record jacket that contains two panels that are folded in half. It is the same size as a standard LP jacket when closed. This not only provides a canvas for extensive art, but it is also typically used to house double LPs. Triple and quad gatefold jackets are also available and are used to house three and four LPs, respectively.

Flipback Jacket

A flipback cover is one that is held together with flaps that fold to the back of the cover from the front, creating a seam.

2LP, 3LP, 4LP Quad LP, Double LP, and More!

Albums are recorded in a variety of lengths. Especially throughout the 1990s and 2000s, artists began recording albums that were lengthier due to the fact that CDs could hold significantly more music than a record. With the resurgence of vinyl, consumers are now demanding releases from the 1990s and 2000s to be pressed to vinyl. The bulk of these albums run longer than 44 minutes (the standard length of a single LP); therefore, recordings often span across various records encased in one package.

- **Single LP:** This is one 12-inch record. If it is a single, meaning not a full-length album, it will be referred to as a 12-inch EP. If a standard full-length album is on just one record, it is often referred to as an LP.
- **Two records:** A double LP is often indicated by either a 2XLP or 2LP. Commonly found for albums originally released through the 1990s to present.
- **Three records:** A triple LP is often indicated by either a 3XLP or 3LP. This is commonly used for lengthy soundtracks or a full-length album accompanying bonus material.
- **Four records:** Often referred to as a quad LP or a 4XLP or 4LP. Not as commonly found, but are typically utilized to showcase bonus material or live performances alongside a full-length release.
- **More than four records:** You can find any number of records contained in one release, and it will use the same format with the number placed before XLP or LP. For example, Mondo released a limited-edition (1,200 copies) *Batman: The Animated Series 8XLP Boxed Set* that contained sixteen full-episode scores on eight 180-gram, 12-inch LPs.

Record Sleeves

Your vinyl should be protected in multiple ways. Protecting the outer jacket as well as the record inside will help preserve the value of your vinyl and keep your collection in good playing condition.

Outer Record Sleeve

This is a plastic sleeve that is placed over the album. New albums are typically shrink-wrapped, and this outer plastic sleeve needs to be purchased separately to protect the jacket once the shrink-wrap is removed. These sleeves play a key role in preserving your collection and are further described in Chapter 8.

Inner Record Sleeve

This is the sleeve the record sits in before it is inserted into its jacket. Records are commonly stored in just a plain paper sleeve, but higher-quality records should be stored in a pol-ylined sleeve. See further details on sleeves in Chapter 8.

Old versus New

Now that you know the lingo, should you buy new or used vinyl? Although millions of records are being pressed each year, not every album is available new . . . and even if it is, there may be earlier pressings out there that deliver higher-quality sound. Used vinyl tends to be lower in price and more readily available, since many vinyl collectors kept their records in exceptional condition. However, with the vinyl boom in full force, finding stacks of used records is not as common as it was in the early 2010s. The value of used records has in-creased significantly—if a stockpile of used vinyl is for sale at a reasonably low rate, it is quickly snatched up by profes-sional record buyers who hunt for records daily.

You should select both new and used vinyl with thought and care. Used vinyl is available in all conditions, but there is nothing worse than buying a used record only to find out when you return home that it is scratched to pieces and unplayable. Even new vinyl occasionally can be damaged! Once in a while new records are scratched, warped, or the jackets are not in acceptable condition. Or you may find a record that appears immaculate, but when you get home it is troublesome to play.

THE TOP-SELLING VINYL IN RECENT TIMES

According to the Official Charts Company, Oasis *(What's the Story) Morning Glory?* was the number one–selling vinyl album between 1993 and 2013.

CHAPTER 6

Purchasing Used Records

*T*he best way to start building a collection is by acquiring a few reasonably priced used records. New records typically cost between $15 and $45, whereas you can buy tons of used records for under $15. Starting with purchasing a few used records that are on the lower end of the price spectrum will help you get comfortable operating a turntable and learning how to handle records before you invest more money in the hobby.

Even the act of buying used records is a skill in itself. You usually can't test the records before you buy them, and used records are commonly not returnable. Before we cover the numerous places to acquire used vinyl, let's review how to inspect used records to ensure that you come home with quality finds.

Examining and Inspecting Used Records

When buying used records, you will probably have to sort through a ton of junk before choosing a quality record. No matter where you sift through used records, whether it be garage sales, thrift shops, or record stores, take your time. Don't be afraid to grab a bunch of records and move aside to examine them individually, choosing only the ones that are in a satisfying condition. Not all records need to be in pristine, mint condition, but you need time to be sure you buy vinyl with a lot of life left in it.

Examining the Packaging

The first component to examine is the condition of the jacket. Here are the issues you may encounter:

1. **Water damage:** If there is water damage on the record jacket, the actual record may have been exposed to water, too. Vinyl with minimal water damage can be used once properly cleaned. However, avoid records that smell musty or moldy.
2. **Jacket wear and tear:** Examine the jacket for various types of wear and tear. Heavily used or improperly stored records will have significant damage to the jacket, such as seam splits, a split on the edge of the jacket, or ring wear (a circular ring that shows up on the jacket when records are stored incorrectly).
3. **Missing inner sleeve:** When properly stored, vinyl records are supposed to sit in an inner sleeve. It doesn't matter as much what type of sleeve as long

as there is one. If there is no inner sleeve, the record was not stored properly and you'll need to carefully inspect the record for damage.

4. **Missing inserts:** If you are considering purchasing a specific release, such as Alice Cooper *School's Out*, which included a report card with track listings as an insert and a pair of paper panties, you should be sure these components are in the used version you're examining. An easy way to get all the information on the contents of a specific pressing is to search a title on Discogs (www.discogs.com), a comprehensive music database.

5. **Markings on the jacket:** This is especially common among used records. Record stores used to place a sticker directly on the jacket or even just wrote the price directly on the cover. People also sometimes wrote their names on their records to know whose was whose. These markings do not diminish sound quality, of course, but are a personal preference to take into account when purchasing.

Unless the goal is to buy and resell the record, or flipping the record, you may not be concerned too much with minor jacket wear and tear and other damage such as markings on the jacket. If you are aiming to land a good-quality record, simply ensure that none of these markings on the jacket indicate potential heavy usage or damage to the actual record itself.

Examining the Record

It is tough to distinguish whether a record has been played on proper equipment and carefully handled, but here are some tips so you can do the best job possible. Try to examine the record in a brightly lit area, preferably using a high-lumen desk lamp or natural sunlight. You can also invest in a miniature magnifying glass with a tiny but bright light for as little as $10. If you spin the record around while in a brightly lit area, the light will reflect off the record, enabling you to identify scratches, scuffs, or other damage. Here are the issues you should watch for:

1. **Correct record:** First and foremost, make sure that the record in the jacket is in fact the correct record. If the album jacket is a gatefold and there is only one record, refer to the center label to verify if a second LP should have been included. You could also enlist Discogs to verify if there should be two LPs.

2. **Scuffs:** Scuffs are usually caused by records rubbing up against something else because they were not properly stored in protective sleeves. Depending on how thick the groove is cut and the weight of the vinyl, these scuffs may affect the way the record plays.

3. **Scratches:** Similar to scuffs, light scratches do not interfere with the sound playback, while deeper scratches will yield a dreadful spinning experience. Scratches that appear in the direction of the groove rather than across it are known as tramlines. These types of scratches are tough to spot but can cause a needle to stick, permanently repeating the groove.

4. **Groove wear:** Groove wear can be difficult to visually detect, but you will hear a distortion in the sound if you're able to play the record. A heavy tracking arm or using a worn-out stylus typically causes groove wear. Visual indications of possible extensive groove wear include a white lining within the groove or a hazy grayish-colored groove.

5. **Needle drop damage:** This occurs when a needle is dropped too heavily onto a record. The start of the first track on all sides (where a needle is typically dropped to start the record) is where damage is likely to occur. This damage can cause clicks and pops. Carefully examine the lead-in groove on either side of the record to locate signs of needle drop damage. If you find any scratches, scuffs, groove wear, or needle drop damage, touch them delicately with your finger to determine how deep the damage is. A seemingly light scuff could turn out to be a deep scratch, which you'll want to avoid.

6. **Center label and spindle hole:** The center hole can indicate how often the record was played. Marks around the hole indicate heavy use. If the spindle hole is misshaped, that will also signify previous record owners played the record often. Scratches on the center label may indicate the previous user had poor eye-hand coordination.

7. **Warped disc:** Heavy warping of a record can indicate possible exposure to heat or that the record was stored improperly (likely flat as opposed to vertically).

You can build a large collection of vinyl on a budget by purchasing used. However, a considerable amount of used vinyl is junk and not worth any money. Focus on figuring out the condition of a record first, and then weigh any damage against the cost of the record. A record may have a few of the issues just mentioned, but at the right price it may be worth it. For example, there is nothing wrong with buying a record for a dollar that has a beat-up jacket if your only intentions are to play it and not resell it.

Grading Used Records

Often used record sellers, such as record shops and thrift and antique stores, will grade records. Grading records allows the seller to obtain a higher price for it while indicating the record's condition to the buyer. If you come across records that are graded, they are likely graded using the Goldmine Grading Guide. Here's how the system works:

- **Still Sealed (SS):** Indicates the record is still sealed. Be wary, though—unscrupulous retailers sometimes just reseal records if they have the equipment to do so. Although it is almost impossible to be 100 percent certain the record was not resealed by a retailer, there are some indicators that may help you decide if it is truly in SS condition. Inspect the record to see if you notice any wear on the jacket, such as tears or scuffs out of the paper. Additionally, if it is still sealed and several years old, it likely could include an original retail pricing or promotional sticker.
- **Mint (M):** These records have never been played and should be sealed. These records are priced at the highest value.
- **Near Mint (NM or M-):** A nearly untouched record that shows no sign of wear and tear. The LP cover should have no creases, seam splits, or other defects. All components should be included and should be in pristine condition.
- **Very Good Plus (VG+):** These records will show minimal sign of handling and/or use. However, it should be apparent that the owner took excellent care of the record. These are generally worth approximately 50 percent of the Near Mint value. Record surface may have minimal signs of wear, such as a slight warp or

scuff or scratches that do not affect the play. Jackets may have a bit of ring wear or slight discoloration, but it should be barely noticeable. The center hole should not be misshaped (that happens with heavy play).

- **Very Good (VG):** Generally worth around 25 percent of the Near Mint value, these records will show heavier signs of usage. Groove wear will also become noticeable. The scratches and scuffs may be faintly apparent when listening to the record. There may be writing or stickers on the jacket.
- **Good (G) and Good Plus (G+):** These records are worth approximately 10–15 percent of the Near Mint value. These records still may play well without skipping, but will have surface noises, scratches, and visible groove wear. The jacket will have seam splits, ring wear, writing, or other damage.

I SEE TWO GRADES!

You might come across a record with two grades—one for the record itself and a one for the jacket. The jacket may be damaged with a Poor (P) rating, but the record is Very Good (VG) condition. If it is an album you want to play but don't necessarily care about the jacket, you could consider buying a generic replacement sleeve. For extensive information on record grading and the value of records, check out the *Goldmine* website: www.Goldminemag.com.

- **Poor (P) or Fair (F):** These records are typically worth 0–5 percent of the Near Mint value. The record can be challenging to play, with frequent skipping or repeating. Vinyl is often crudely warped or cracked. Jackets can be water damaged, heavily damaged, or even missing!

- **Virgin vinyl:** Every now and again, you will come across an unopened, unused record, which is referred to as virgin vinyl. There is nothing as exciting as coming across a virgin vinyl record while hunting, but be aware that irresponsible retailers can shrink-wrap opened records.

Where to Buy Used Vinyl

A thrilling aspect of collecting is the process of digging for the records to add to your collection. Often, used records are the only way to acquire certain titles because they may be out of print, meaning no current copies are being produced. Following are some stops you might want to make on your journey to build your vinyl collection.

Local Record Shops

Experienced used record collectors shop often, some weekly, and others (remarkably) almost daily! Good records don't stay on the shelf for a long time, so frequent visits to your local record shop will increase your likelihood of finding gems.

Spending a good amount of time at the local record store will also enable you to build relationships with the staff. They are likely avid record collectors and can help you find the records you desire. At my Niagara Falls store, I look forward to seeing several customers who visit the store each week at the same time. Most of them easily spend an hour plus chatting with the staff, exploring records together. At a quality local record store, you should feel comfortable spending a lot of time there and feel at ease asking questions.

A shellac record

Edison's cylinders

Herb Alpert and the Tijuana Brass's 1965 release *Whipped Cream & Other Delights*

The Beatles's *The White Album*

Led Zeppelin III

✎ Outer sleeve, jacket, inner sleeve, vinyl

✎ Promotional record

N Nirvana's *Nevermind*

N Fugees' *The Score*

↗ Blink-182's *Take Off Your Pants and Jacket*

↗ David Bowie's *Reality*

Jack White's *Live at Third Man Records*

Jack White's *Lazaretto*

A liquid-filled *Aliens* soundtrack

Garage and Estate Sales

Shopping at both garage and estate sales is a great way to add to your record collection—if you know how to approach them. Here are tips for shopping at both estate and garage sales:

1. **Generate a plan:** If you're planning multiple stops, make a plan before you leave the house. The website www.estatesales.net lists upcoming estate sales throughout the United States. Garage sale listings can be found on websites such as Craigslist and Kijiji and on local Facebook forums. In some instances, these listings can indicate what categories of vinyl they will be selling, allowing you to prioritize which ones to hit up first, based on your interests.
2. **Set a budget and bring cash:** Garage and estate sales are almost always cash only. Setting a budget beforehand will help you avoid purchasing unnecessary stuff. That said, consider bringing additional cash just in case you find an amazing rarity. Infrequently, garage and estate sales accept credit or debit cards . . . but even if they do, cash is always better if you are negotiating.
3. **Inspect the records:** Using the methods mentioned earlier in this chapter, inspect the records to determine if the conditions of the records are acceptable before you decide what you are willing to pay for the records.
4. **Negotiate:** Records at garage and estate sales should be significantly cheaper than those at a local record shop. Don't be afraid to politely request a lower price than the one indicated.

5. **Consider buying a large quantity:** Remember the goal of estate and garage sales is to get rid of as much stuff as possible. Therefore, you might be able to score an exceptional deal if you offer to buy a bunch of records instead of just one or two. If you buy a large quantity of records, but only want to keep a few titles, your local record shop may be inclined to purchase the remainder. This is an excellent strategy when the seller is motivated to sell all the records, versus the few you may be interested in. Try this method if you are at a busy garage sale and do not have time to rummage through the records before others grab up records you haven't had a chance to look at.

Thrift and Antique Stores

I have noticed in the last few years that with the increase of vinyl sales, thrift and antique stores are starting to individually grade and price records higher than ever, especially within metropolitan areas. Chain thrift stores are also starting to recognize the demand for vinyl and have increased their prices. That doesn't necessarily imply that you'll never find a good deal at one of these spots, but be cautious. Many antique dealers focus on items that have higher price points and may not pay too much attention to pricing their vinyl.

An excellent thrift and antique shopping strategy is to visit often and to earn the friendship of the dealers. Avid record collectors visit the chain thrift stores with donation boxes almost daily! Because antique shops usually do not accept donations, they tend to obtain stock less often, and a weekly or biweekly visit may be sufficient. Once again, becoming friends with the thrift and antique dealers will provide an advantage, and they can likely provide an idea as to how often they bring in stock.

Clever antique and thrift store owners will now look online for pricing guidelines before putting vinyl out for sale. Even charitable thrift stores realize they should glance online for the value of a record before placing it out for sale, so it's harder than ever to find a gem for a steal.

BE SURE TO NEGOTIATE!
Vendors at record shows are often willing to negotiate, so you might be able to haggle deals.

Record Shows

Record shows are events where groups of record vendors come together in various cities across the world to sell vinyl. While select vendors sell new records, a large amount of them sell older, used vinyl. Record shows were quite popular among collectors before the current vinyl boom happened. Not too long ago, there was a shortage of retail outlets to purchase vinyl. Chain retailers were not selling records and there weren't nearly as many independent record stores around, either. These shows brought together nearby vendors to provide record collectors a chance to do some extensive shopping.

Record shows usually occur in hotels, churches, schools, and other temporary rented facilities. Although the majority of products for sale at these shows are records, often other vendors with unique music-related products and memorabilia are included. These events are also a way to connect with other vinyl collectors within your area. They are a truly enjoyable and unique experience.

Record shows usually charge a nominal entrance fee. To find out about record shows in your area, visit your local record shop and ask about any upcoming events.

Purchasing Used Vinyl Online

There are quite a few ways to purchase used vinyl on the Internet. Here are a few spots that collectors find reputable.

Discogs

Discogs is not just a website; it is the world's largest music database and marketplace with more than 7.1 million titles listed. The content within the Discogs database is completely user generated and is updated constantly. Discogs is an excellent tool to use while hunting for used records. Discogs provides a pricing scale that accumulates the history of sales for every item on the site and highlights the lowest price, the median (average), and the highest price each item has ever sold for. This information gives you a clear indication as to what a record is worth. Additionally, if you download the free Discogs app, you can use your cell phone camera to scan the barcode on the record jacket and instantly locate the item within the Discogs marketplace. If a barcode is not available, you can enter the catalog number into Discogs to directly link to the item.

Discogs is also a marketplace that connects buyers with sellers from all over the world, to facilitate shopping for both discount and rare records. Records on Discogs are graded using the Goldmine Grading Guide. Buyers also rate their experience with sellers, allowing you to easily pinpoint how reputable they are. A seller's location is provided so you can estimate shipping properly. All payments for Discogs sales are made through PayPal, and the seller has to provide PayPal with tracking information for your package. PayPal employs a buyer-supportive return policy, and it is likely if something goes wrong they will assist you. PayPal also offers a 180-day dispute timeframe in case the records are not received.

eBay

Comparable to Discogs, eBay provides a consumer-to-consumer sales forum. However, on eBay you are *bidding* on the records, whereas Discogs sellers list a set price. eBay is primarily utilized to sell valuable records as opposed to the cheaper stuff. eBay is also a good spot to find larger collections at a discount price.

PAY ATTENTION TO PACKAGING
When purchasing on eBay and Discogs, do not be afraid to confirm with the seller the type of packaging they will use to ship records. It is imperative that a seller properly packages the records to avoid any damage during shipping.

eBay does not provide a pricing guideline or history for the sale of its items directly, but you can visit Popsike (www.popsike.com) to view sales history on a specific item. If you type an album title into Popsike, it will show the various sales that have occurred for that specific item, including the prices they were sold at and the dates they were sold. This tool ensures that you are paying a fair price for records on eBay.

Similar to Discogs, eBay is a middleman and does not directly sell items. The sellers are rated by the buyers and vice versa, and sellers can provide feedback in regards to their experience. eBay offers a way to initiate a dispute with a seller if an issue arises. Using PayPal for all your eBay purchases will also ensure protection.

Classified Advertisements

Those who decide to no longer collect vinyl or those who have inherited a collection of records they don't want often advertise records locally through classified ads. There are traditional print classifieds within newspapers and other local print papers in addition to online classified advertising. Although there are not usually many print ads for used records, I have found when there are, the prices are reasonable in comparison to those online. Two magnificent online sources to locate used vinyl in your area are the local listings on Craigslist (www.craigslist.org) in the United States and Kijiji (www.kijiji.ca) in Canada.

CHAPTER 7

Purchasing New Vinyl

*T*here are endless places to purchase new vinyl nowadays. After all, more than 17 million records were manufactured and sold in 2015! There is a plethora of places to find vinyl, including local record stores, big-box retailers that are now selling vinyl (such as Whole Foods and even Cracker Barrel), online stores, and more.

New Vinyl–Specific Considerations

Here are key things to know when purchasing new vinyl:

1. **Exclusives:** With the popularity of vinyl releases and reissues, countless titles are being pressed on multiple colored variants available exclusively only through certain retailers, and frequently through the artists' websites directly. If you hear about a current record in a particular color variant, be sure to verify where this item is available before heading out to just any record shop.

2. **Pops and skips:** When purchasing new vinyl, if issues occur with the way the record sounds, such as pops and skips, but scratches are not detected, clean your record before attempting to replay it. Don't assume the record is unusable and needs to be returned. At times, even new records collect dust while in the factory. Sometimes residue from the pressing process is left on the record. If the issue is residue on the record from the pressing process, either using a proper cleaning method (see Chapter 9) or playing the record a few times is the best way to get rid of this (the stylus will cut through dust and clean the grooves). Remember, turntables *and* records can be finicky, so refer to Chapter 9 and learn a how to clean a record before continuing to play.

3. **Ordering online and shipping:** There is nothing more heartbreaking than waiting for a record delivery and finding upon arrival that it is packaged in materials clearly not suitable for protecting the record. If purchasing new vinyl online, make sure the sender uses

protective mailers. Records are commonly damaged beyond repair during shipping if not properly packaged. They can be warped, the jackets can be destroyed, mailing can cause seam splits, and of course the record can be cracked in half if not properly packaged. Luckily, sturdy LP mailers exist, and reputable online sources use them.

Where to Buy New Vinyl

With the increased demand for vinyl, it is occasionally difficult to secure copies of new releases and reissues, even with the variety of places to buy records nowadays. Following, I have provided details not only on all the different types of places to score new vinyl, but have included a collection of tips on how to score the scarcer and limited stuff you might want to add to your collection.

Independent Record Stores

The independent, or indie, record store is an independently owned, local brick-and-mortar record store that is not affiliated with a big-box chain brand. Over the last fifteen years, major music retail chains have dwindled and gone out of business, while the amount of independently owned record stores has grown. Independent stores are more of a community rather than just a regular retail store. Frequently, indie stores are closely connected with artists and labels, providing relationships that are rewarding for the consumer. Music is supposed to be entertaining, and quality indie retailers keep it that way.

Indie retail store staff often have the same passion for music as their customers. A really good indie store will know their regular customers and will work with you to get the records you need. My number one suggestion for buying vinyl is build a relationship with your indie store, because they will be the ones to help you collect both the basics and the difficult-to-find rarities.

Vinyl and Major Retailers

The early 2000s was a tough time for music, notably for physical media. The Internet made digital music pirating effortless, which contributed significantly to dwindling sales. But that was not the music industry's only issue. Mass discount retailers such as major chain grocery stores like Walmart and online stores such as Amazon were selling CDs at a margin that music-specific retailers could not compete with.

By 2006, major music retailers such as Tower Records, Sam Goody, and Musicland began to downsize and close. Tower Records entered bankruptcy for the first time in 2004 and again in 2006. In October 2006, the Great American Group acquired Tower's assets and liquidated the following day, and going-out-of-business sales occurred all across the United States, with the last location shutting its doors on December 22, 2006.

The Musicland Group, an entertainment group that included the Sam Goody, Musicland, and Media Play music retail brands, also suffered throughout the 2000s. In 2001, Best Buy acquired the Musicland Group and within a few years sold it to Sun Capital Partners. In January 2006, Musicland Group filed for Chapter 11 bankruptcy and began closing Sam Goody stores in February of that same year. In March 2006, Trans World Entertainment purchased Musicland. They converted a portion of the Sam Goody stores into F.Y.E. stores, a retail mall chain in the United States.

Only a few music-specific retail chains still exist, including F.Y.E. in the United States and HMV in Canada and the United Kingdom.

Other Chain Retailers Selling Vinyl

The majority of chain retailers that currently sell vinyl are not music specific and include companies that would surprise you with their vinyl selection, including Whole Foods and Cracker Barrel! Here are worthwhile retailers to hit up for vinyl.

URBAN OUTFITTERS
Clothing retailer Urban Outfitters currently stocks a fairly generous selection of vinyl. They carry a mixture of both new releases and reissues spanning a range of genres such as classic rock, indie, hip-hop, rock, and more. They also offer a commendable array of titles in colors exclusively available through their stores.

BARNES & NOBLE
Best known for book sales, Barnes & Noble is now also an excellent source for new records. Their record section is set up similarly to what you used to experience within traditional music retail stores, and they offer a diverse selection of vinyl spanning a variety of genres.

NEWBURY COMICS
Both a music and comic book retailer, Newbury Comics is an excellent store for vinyl, particularly for limited vinyl only available through them. They currently stock a huge selection of records on color variants available only at their

twenty-eight retail stores and on their website. Cherished Newbury exclusives include the Pearl Jam *Ten* vinyl on a Coke bottle clear variant, which is limited to 2,000 copies; The Strokes *Is This It* blue and gold colored vinyl, limited to 1,000 copies; and Nirvana *Bleach* on red and black swirled vinyl, limited to 750 copies. Each of these titles is out of print and has a resale value of over $100.

WHOLE FOODS, CRACKER BARREL, AND MORE

As vinyl rebounded, a few unexpected retailers began stocking vinyl. In 2013, Whole Foods launched a vinyl record section alongside its sale of organic vegetables. In the United Kingdom, several retail chains tried out the sale of records alongside their other products, such as Gap and grocery stores Tesco and Aldi. In early 2016, the U.S. restaurant chain Cracker Barrel entered the vinyl market with an exclusive numbered release of Joey + Rory *Hymns That Are Important to Us*.

Online Retailers

Online stores are one of the most popular ways to obtain vinyl. Prior to the vinyl rebound, a considerable number of major brick-and-mortar retailers were hesitant to stock vinyl and primarily sold CDs. Online was a way to offer vinyl to the market without large investments in stock and shelf space. A generous fraction of vinyl released prior to the revival was done through do-it-yourself niche sites, the artist directly, and Amazon.

Amazon

Although online only, Amazon (www.amazon.com) is the single largest retailer of vinyl with approximately 12 percent of the market share as of 2014. Amazon is a straightforward retailer to purchase vinyl from. They offer free two-day shipping for Amazon Prime members, have the largest selection available, and often carry quite a bit of stock. Amazon also allows others to sell through their site, similar to eBay and Discogs, so it can also be used as a way to obtain out-of-print, new, and used vinyl through third-party sellers.

Artist Exclusives

Artists now sell exclusive vinyl variants directly to their fans from their websites or on their tours. A lot of artists offer vinyl new releases or album reissues directly through their own website. When scoping out a new release, it is always wise to check the artist's website to see if they will be offering a limited color, autographed copies, or additional bonus items that you can purchase directly through them.

Independent Online Retailers

Equivalent to the indie brick-and-mortar retailers, several independent vinyl web stores exist. Here are a few of the major online vinyl retailers that are reliable and excellent to shop with:

ACOUSTIC SOUNDS

Acoustic Sounds (www.acousticsounds.com) is an online business that specializes in the sale of audiophile vinyl, SACDs, DVD-Audio, and high-quality equipment. Launched in 1986,

Acoustic Sounds started off as a mail-order business from the founder's (Chad Kassem) apartment and has grown into one of the largest online suppliers of vinyl, specifically audiophile and collectible records. In 2010, Acoustic Sounds also launched their own pressing plant, Quality Record Pressings (QRP), allowing them to further control and improve the quality of their releases. The Acoustic Sounds website currently has a large selection of reissues exclusively released by them in addition to audiophile records from other labels. The website also has a "vault" section that includes rare and valuable records.

SOUNDSTAGE DIRECT

SoundStage Direct (www.soundstagedirect.com), which is an excellent resource for turntables, also carries a diverse selection of new vinyl. SoundStage Direct is extremely reliable and are undoubtedly passionate about what they do. When heading over to their website, check out their page that shows how carefully they package their records. Sound-Stage Direct has excellent customer service as well.

SRCVINYL

The store I currently own, SRCVinyl (www.srcvinyl.com), is a one-stop shop for new, unopened vinyl that ships from both Canada and the United States. My spouse, Danny Keyes, and I accidently started SRCVinyl in 2006 when our already struggling business, an online radio station PunkRadioCast, was thrown under by the recession. This was the year a tremendous number of music retailers went under, including Sam Goody and Tower Records. Every single one of our advertisers dropped us in the same week and we were required to act quickly. A record label–owning friend of ours suggested that we might stay in business for a few months if we traded ads in exchange for CDs and records. PunkRadioCast had a large audience who were passionate about music; therefore, selling product was fairly simple.

After doing this for a few months, we recognized that quite a few record labels and distributors had stock vinyl that were highly sought after by niche communities of record collectors. One of the ways we connected to those collectors was through a free web community, Vinyl Collective (www .vinylcollective.com), which we eventually acquired. The early SRCVinyl years mainly consisted of us finding and buying records that the industry typically labeled "dead stock" but were actually highly sought after.

By 2012, we became acquainted with what records collectors wanted and as a result developed relationships with a variety of record labels and began reissuing records that were in demand but not available on vinyl. SRCVinyl exists today as a vinyl-centric online store with a catalog of more than 5,000 new vinyl available at any given time, including a large selection of exclusive titles and color variants.

Vinyl Subscriptions

These types of music services have been around since 1955, when Columbia Records launched its Columbia Record Club, later renamed Columbia House. Columbia House sold music to consumers through direct mail, and all titles made available through the subscription were at least six months old. The service was launched to provide consumers living in rural areas who did not have access to brick-and-mortar stores a way to purchase albums. By 1956, the subscription service had sold 7 million records. Fast-forward to 2015: after Columbia House was sold and downsized several times throughout the 2000s, it was sold off through a bankruptcy auction in 2015 to its current owner, John Lippman.

He hinted in December 2015 that Columbia House will re-launch as a vinyl subscription service.

A handful of records, many that have gone on to sell for quite high prices, were originally available through vinyl subscriptions and fan clubs. Sub Pop Records launched a singles club that featured 7-inch singles. The first set was issued from November 1988 to December 1993, the second between April 1998 and March 2002, and the third between August 2008 and October 2009. The debut single was Nirvana's "Love Buzz b/w Big Cheese." This 7-inch single was limited to 1,000 copies and has a median selling price of $1,770 on the Discogs website.

Third Man Records, the record label of Jack White of The White Stripes, has had its popular Vault subscription service since 2009. Each quarter, subscribers receive an exclusive Vault LP, a Vault 7-inch, and a bonus item that has included T-shirts, posters, postcards, and DVDs. The first Vault package was a mono version of The White Stripes album *Icky Thump*, which has sold for as high as $499. The latest, Vault package 29, includes the LP a live-to-acetate recording of Pearl Jam recorded at the Third Man Records studio, a solo acoustic recording of Eddie Vedder as the 7-inch, and Pearl Jam at Third Man Records pin, patch, and photo album as the bonus items. A subscription costs $60/quarter, and extra perks include a 10 percent discount at the Third Man Records store and a 75 percent discount on a Tidal subscription.

Another vinyl subscription service, Vinyl Me, Please (www.vinylmeplease.com), sends subscribers a new or reissued exclusive album every month. Subscribers, however, don't get to choose what is sent. Cost as of this writing was $23/month.

Unlike Vinyl Me, Please, the subscription service VNYL (www.vnyl.org) sends their subscribers a monthly shipment of 1–3 records, curated specifically for them based on information provided. Subscriptions are $22/month for one record and

$39/month for three records ($37/month for a three-month subscription and $35/month for a one-year subscription).

Bootleg Records

A bootleg or unofficial record is an album that is not officially released by the artist or record label. Bootleg records can consist of either an illegally duplicated album or an illegally recorded live performance that is sold and circulated on vinyl. Although bootleggers financially profit from the sale of these records, the label and the artist never earn a dime. One way the industry combated bootlegs was by immediately releasing the same album officially. If the official version was produced with improved quality, this would decrease the demand for the bootleg and would essentially cease the production of the bootleg.

Bootlegs are no longer produced in the numbers that they once were, so don't worry about a newly manufactured product being a bootleg. With the scarcity of record-pressing machines, there is not enough equipment available to produce bootlegs. However, with older titles, bootleg versions are likely to exist. If you are ever unsure if an album you are interested in is a bootleg, here are a few ways to verify:

- Check that the record is shrink-wrapped and sealed.
- Check the album for a catalog number, logos from the record label, and legal copy indicating who released and distributed it. Bootleggers do not include this detailed information.
- Check Discogs; they list if a pressing is official or not.
- If purchasing on eBay, make sure the seller shows pictures of the item before buying. Don't be afraid if you are in doubt to confirm with the seller that it is not a bootleg.

CHAPTER 8

Storing Records

*S*toring records requires a bit of thought and care. This chapter covers everything you need to know to handle and store your vinyl so that your records are protected. I'll also provide advice on insuring your collection—something people often don't realize they can do until it's too late.

How to Properly Handle a Record

One of the best ways to preserve and store your collection is to make sure you are carefully handling your records. Here's the procedure you should use to remove a record from a jacket and how to properly place it back into the jacket.

Removing a Record from Its Jacket

1. Wash your hands before handling records. Some collectors even prefer to wear a pair of clean, lint-free white gloves while handling records.
2. Don't have food or drink near records and turntable.
3. Never touch the area on the record that has grooves with your hands. When touching a record, you should touch either the edge of the record or the center label.
4. To remove a record from the jacket, open the jacket and carefully pull out the record's inner sleeve. Avoid touching the actual record within the sleeve if possible.
5. To remove the record from the inner sleeve, open the inner sleeve and let the record slide into an open hand. When it touches your hand, the edge of the record should touch your thumb and you should be able to touch the center label with your middle finger.

Storing a Record After You Play It

1. After playing a record, clean it (using one of the methods we discuss next) to make sure no dust or dirt is stored within the record groove.

2. Place the record back in its inner sleeve by bowing open the inner sleeve and carefully *sliding* the record back into the sleeve. *Never* drop a record into its inner sleeve.
3. Place the album jacket into the plastic outer sleeve.
4. Place the record that is now housed in its inner sleeve behind the album jacket, between the jacket and the outer sleeve. Storing your record in its inner sleeve only, outside the jacket, will guarantee you do not seam split your jacket and prevents ring wear, increasing the likelihood of keeping both the album and jacket in a pristine condition.

Following are some other dos and don'ts:

- **Don't leave your records outside the sleeve:** When finished playing your records, be sure to store them inside an inner sleeve. Records scratch easily and collect dust. Storing the records in their sleeve is the best method to protect the record.
- **Do not stack vinyl records:** Do not store records flat, and never stack records on top of each other. This can cause warping, ring wear, and scratches. Records should be stored standing up on a shelf or other suitable storage.
- **Always use a cueing lever:** When playing a record, always drop the needle to the record with the cueing lever! If you drop your needle onto the record, it can damage both the record and the stylus.

Proper Methods for Storing Your Collection

One of the most common ways records become damaged is from improper storage or mishandling. Here are fundamental points to remember when choosing how and where to store your records:

- **Avoid direct sunlight:** UV rays can cause discoloring of the record jacket. Additionally, records themselves are extremely sensitive to intense heat. With exposure to extremely hot, direct sunlight, records can warp and even melt! If you purchase records online, consider ways to avoid possible heat exposure. If you are not home when a package is delivered, the delivery person will often place your package outside anywhere that is convenient. During the hot months, I ensure my records are delivered to my workplace or I leave a note for the carrier to place the records in a specific place that will be away from direct sunlight.
- **Avoid heat:** Sunlight is not the only source of heat damaging to records. Be sure not to store too close to a radiator or vent that may produce high levels of heat. Records should be stored at or below room temperature.
- **Avoid extreme cold:** Moderate coolness does not cause damage to records, but extreme cold (below freezing point) can cause records to warp if not stored properly or if they are brought back to room temperature too quickly. If you ever move records from an extremely cool temperature to room temperature, be sure to allow them to acclimatize before handling to avoid warping.

- **Store records in an upright position:** It is imperative to store your records in an upright, vertical position and never lay them flat or on top of each other. Do not store them upright on an angle; that can also warp the record. Store them completely vertical or on a minimal angle. There are various options for storing your records in an upright position (more on that later in this chapter).

- **Store in a relatively dry area:** Be sure your records are stored in a room that has a relative humidity of 35–40 percent. Storing them in a basement, especially a wet or musty basement, can be harmful to the records. You should also avoid attics, garages, or sheds because they tend to be fairly moist. Moisture is damaging to both the record jacket and vinyl. Additionally, if a room is extremely dry, the record jackets can get brittle and the LPs can get damaged. If you are limited to an area with either too moist or dry conditions, you can invest in either a humidifier or dehumidifier to control the amount of moisture in the room.

- **Record sleeves:** Always store your records in proper inner and outer sleeves. Proper sleeves are the best way to both protect and retain a clean collection.

WHAT HAPPENS WHEN YOU FREEZE RECORDS?
Discogs member AMJacker decided to conduct and video an experiment to determine how cold records can get before they break and warp. Using his workplace lab, he froze records to –112°F and –265°F and then brought them back up to room temperature quickly. Check out the the experiment here: https://youtube/8HwjBFH3AMM.

152 Record Sleeves

In order to properly store a record and keep it in the best condition possible you need an outer sleeve, typically made out of plastic, and an inner sleeve, typically made out of paper or a paper and plastic combination. Outer sleeves are placed over your jacket to protect your records from dust and dirt. They also act as a barrier, protecting your record jackets from damage, even when storing them. If you store records on a shelf without sleeves on them, damage will occur from rubbing against each other while pulling them in and out, in addition to deteriorating from sitting up against other records.

WHERE TO BUY RECORD SLEEVES
Record inner and outer sleeves can be purchased at independent record stores or online at the indie record stores mentioned: Acoustic Sounds, SoundStage Direct, and SRCVinyl. If you are considering purchasing larger quantities of sleeves, in excess of a few hundred, an excellent source is Bags Unlimited (www.bagsunlimited.com), an online retailer from Rochester, New York, that offers protection supplies of all sorts. I have purchased more than 50,000 sleeves from Bags Unlimited and they are extremely reliable and pleasant to shop with.

Inner sleeves are the sleeves you place the LP inside. Proper inner sleeves protect the actual LPs from dust and dirt while also protecting them from getting scratched while stored. There are several different types of both inner and outer sleeves available on the market. Let's explore the available sleeve types individually, so you can purchase what's right for you.

Outer Sleeves

Outer sleeves are made out of plastic, typically polyethylene, polypropylene, polyvinyl, or polyester. They are available in a variety of thicknesses, measured in mils.

POLYPROPYLENE SLEEVES
Average cost per 100 sleeves: $20

These sleeves are significantly thinner and are crystal clear in comparison to polyethylene sleeves. These are generally only available in thinner mils, such as 1.5, and tend to rip quite easily. Due to the fact that they are fairly thin, they are best suited for shorter-term storage. They also have a perfectly clear and shiny appearance to them and therefore are useful for any record covers you wish to display. Polypropylene sleeves are reasonably priced.

POLYETHYLENE SLEEVES
*Most recommended
Average cost per 100 sleeves: $22

These are the most commonly available and used sleeves. Polyethylene sleeves are made for the primary record sizes of 7, 10, and 12 inches, with thickness options typically varying from 2.5 to 6 mils. The higher the number of thickness, the sturdier the sleeves are and the longer they last. The 3-mil polyethylene sleeves are what you usually find on records and most commonly used by record collectors. These are available either with an opening at the top or with a resealable flap. If you can confirm the polyethylene sleeves are made using 100 percent virgin polyethylene, they will not yellow or crack over time. On average, polyethylene sleeves cost roughly $22 per 100 sleeves. These sleeves are best suited for long-term preservation of your collection.

POLYVINYL

Average cost per 100 sleeves: $110

Polyvinyl sleeves are especially thick and durable. Although their durability is a protective feature, an issue with polyvinyl sleeves is that, over time or with exposure to heat or when stored for a long period of time, the sleeves can stick to the cover of the jacket, ruining the cover art. These sleeves are best for short-term storage such as displaying a record or for shipping an item.

POLYESTER SLEEVES

Polyester sleeves, also referred to as Mylar sleeves, are the most durable and are crystal clear. They are available in both 2-mil and 4-mil thicknesses. Polyester sleeves are the only sleeve recognized by the Library of Congress for archiving vinyl records. This is the ultimate sleeve for both preserving and protecting your collection, but they are significantly more expensive than other sleeves.

Inner Sleeves

Standard paper inner sleeves that records are routinely housed in are considered low-quality inner sleeves and can be damaging to your record. They:

- Often turn yellow fairly quickly
- Add static to the record
- Can leave little flakes of paper on the record
- Are typically not made of acid-free paper

Moving the record in and out of these standard paper sleeves is often the culprit of the scuff marks you see on records. To illustrate just how easily this type of paper sleeve damages your record, while you are out shopping grab a $1 record you do not intend on falling in love with. Move the record in and out of the sleeve and you will hear how rough it is on the record and possibly even be able to view how damaging it can be to vinyl. Following are the different types of inner sleeves.

ACID-FREE PAPER
Average cost per 100 sleeves: $20
Paper sleeves are cost-effective, but they provide the least amount of protection for your records. Although they cover the record and protect from dirt and dust, paper can scratch the record. If you elect to house your records in paper sleeves, ensure it is acid-free paper.

POLYETHYLENE
Average cost per 100 sleeves: $20
Polyethylene sleeves are soft and the least damaging to records. They are available in either a low-density version, which is created from low-static polyethylene, or a high-density version, which is made from pure antistatic polyethylene. Due to their soft properties, they will not scratch your records or introduce static, maintaining your records in tip-top shape. One issue with these sleeves is that the plastic is flimsy, causing them to bunch up when inside your record jacket. Round-bottom versions, as opposed to the typical square shapes, are available that reduce the bunching effect.

ACID-FREE POLYLINED
Average cost per 100 Sleeves: $40
This is a paper sleeve with a polylining on the inside. They provide the same sturdiness as paper sleeves, but the

soft, smooth polylining on the inside prevents the scratching that paper can cause.

PAPER-LINED POLY (RICE PAPER SLEEVE)
*Most recommended
Average cost per 100 sleeves: $50

Paper-lined poly sleeves are often referred to by a few names, including high-density polyethylene sleeves, HDPE sleeves, or rice paper sleeves. These sleeves are similar, in terms of quality, to polyethylene sleeves, except they consist of three layers of high-density, antistatic polyethylene and a single sheet of acid-free paper. The acid-free paper enables the sleeve to be sturdy and eliminates the bunching issue. The acid-free paper that is included is sandwiched in between two of the three layers of polyethylene, making sure that the paper never comes into direct contact with the record.

Record Storage Ideas

There are a variety of record-specific storage options that allow you to both store and display your records. Following are a few of the most commonly used record storage options. However, you can be inventive and find endless original possibilities, too. No matter what type of record storage you choose, be sure to consider the following:

- How many records can it hold and will that be enough?
- What size is it and will it fit where I want it to go?
- Will records properly sit vertically within the selected storage option?
- Does it offer any protection from the sun?

- Do I need any portable record storage for traveling with my albums?
- Do I need to find a storage solution that will fit with my style?

Keeping these questions in mind will assure you select the right record storage for you.

Record Carrying Case

A record carrying case is a box that includes a handle and closure, perfectly sized for storing records. They are usually available for 12-, 10- and 7-inch records. Although this type of storage is best suited for a collection of a few records or for transporting records, it is one of the best ways to store records because it is a closed case, protecting your collection from UV rays, dust, and any other contaminants in your environment. Record carrying cases have existed for years, and uniquely retro cases can be found used on eBay or in antique shops for a fairly reasonable price.

Milk Crates

Vintage milk crates are a classic way to store vinyl records. In fact, this method was so popular that milk companies modified their crate size to try to deter people from stealing their crates for record storage. This has made it quite difficult to find used milk crates that are wide enough for storing records.

In some states, it is actually illegal to sell or be in possession of a milk crate bearing a company name that is not yours. Milk crate theft is extremely serious—to the point where a website, Got Milk Crates? (www.gotmilkcrates.com), was set up as a service of the International Dairy Foods Association to deter the unauthorized possession of milk crates! The intention of milk crates is to allow the dairy industry to transport and deliver milk to convenience stores in an environmentally friendly way. Often convenience stores leave their milk crates outside, allowing the milk delivery person to easily access them. According to Got Milk Crates?, the crates are not primarily stolen for personal home use but are often stolen by other businesses for use within the restaurant and catering industry. A plastic milk crate can also yield up to $4 a crate when sold to scrap recyclers, which definitely aids in the milk crate theft issue. Due to the high number of thefts, various states have imposed laws deeming not only the theft of milk crates illegal, but improperly using them, damaging them, and being in illegal possession of a milk crate can land you in serious trouble.

The good news is that there are crates currently being manufactured that can be purchased legally! The storage company Sterilite currently has two styles of crates that fit both LPs and 7-inch records. These are commonly found at both Walmart and Target stores during the summer months alongside their college storage displays. They are also available through SRCVinyl here: www.srcvinyl.com/accessories/storage.html.

Other Storage Crates

Although milk crates are the staple record-storage crate, there are various other types of boxes and crates available at a reasonable price point. Over the last few years, wooden vintage fruit and wine crates have become quite popular and are readily available at garage sales, flea markets, and antique shops. I have lucked out and acquired wooden antique fruit crates that hold 50–100 records for as little as $5! Not to mention, they make for an authentic and appealing decor. If you want to try other types of crates, just be sure they adequately fit the records and support them in standing in an upright position, and be sure the wood is in solid condition with no nails or wood chunks sticking out.

Wax Stacks

These are interlocking, collapsible, and customizable record storage bins, similar to crates. No tools are required—you can build these crates in less than a minute by clicking together interlocking pieces. Wax Stacks crates hold about fifty records and are a bit on the pricier side, at $95 a piece. However, they are worth the money if you can afford them. The crate is stackable, will protect your records while transporting them, and are made from high-quality and sustainable Baltic birch logs.

Record Storage Furniture

A variety of record storage furniture is available ranging from large entertainment units to side tables with slots for storing records. Since vinyl was the primary medium prior to the 1980s, you can often purchase used furniture designed to hold records for reasonable prices at antique shops, thrift stores, garage sales, and on local websites such as Craigslist.

Newly designed and manufactured record storage furniture does exist as well. Here are various reliable sources for record storage furniture:

IKEA Expedit/Kallax

For countless years the IKEA Expedit, a cubby-type bookcase shelving system that perfectly fit records, has been a staple piece of record furniture among record collectors. Boasting the ability to hold around 90–100 records per cubby and available in up to twenty-cubby units, the Expedit was a cost-efficient way to store and display your extensive record collection. The Expedit contained either four, eight, sixteen, or twenty cubbies. You could pair them up, store vertically or horizontally, or in extreme cases stack them twenty cubbies high (while modified to be bolted to a wall, of course).

In 2014, IKEA discontinued the Expedit. Vinyl collectors went crazy and an Internet fury was launched! Immediately, Expedits were sold out all across North America and other countries. I will admit, with news of this I did quickly purchase an entire pallet of these shelves (which I still store in a safe and secure, secret location for future use). Alongside the announcement, IKEA introduced the Kallax, their updated cubby shelf system that has slimmer and sleek edges, as opposed to the sharp edges of the Expedit. Critics of the revised Kallax shelf swore the updated models would be of cheaper quality; however, IKEA notes it has the same properties as the Expedit and can handle the same weight, about 28 pounds per shelf. I own a couple Kallax shelves and have experienced no issues. I am confident the quality is comparable to the Expedit, if not identical.

Urban Outfitters

Urban Outfitters is a tremendous resource for stylish and retro record storage furniture. They carry charming wood media consoles that can hold both records and turntables, in addition to sleek metal record racks. Their online store showcases several different consoles that can accommodate both LPs and your turntable.

Record Frames

Records can be stored and displayed within a record frame. There are a substantial amount of record frames available on the market. When purchasing a frame, be sure that it will not damage the record in any way, unless your goal is solely to display the record and not play it. When using a record frame for a long period of time, consider you are potentially exposing the cover of the record to direct UV light while the rest of the album is covered. If you leave the record in the display frame for quite a while, the cover may discolor. Preservation display frames, which contain museum glass, are available. If you come across a preservation display frame, verify that the museum glass is UV blocking; this will guarantee your cover is protected from any potential UV damage.

DIY RECORD STORAGE IDEAS

Ideas and possibilities for storing records are endless. Modern products are constantly being released. Original do-it-yourself ideas are born every day! If you are contemplating an artsy or unique setup or if you are handy, be sure to check out the following Etsy search for ideas: www.etsy.com/ca/market/record_storage. Or follow me on the Vinyl Collective Pinterest where I constantly add unique and original record storage ideas to my record storage board: www.pinterest.com/vinylcollective/.

Insuring Your Record Collection

As you build your collection, you may reach a point where you knowingly or unknowingly accumulate a valuable stash of records. At that point, you want to be sure to insure them. There is nothing more horrifying than coming home to find all the contents of your home stolen, or experiencing a horrific tragedy such as a fire or flood and losing personal property— so consider giving yourself some peace of mind when it comes to your vinyl collection.

THE WORLD'S LARGEST RECORD COLLECTION
Zero Freitas of Brazil is recognized as the owner of the world's largest record collection, at over 6 million records. Many long-term collectors may recognize him by his anonymous advertisements in *Billboard* magazine that read "RECORD COLLECTIONS. We BUY any record collection. Any style of music. We pay HIGHER prices than anyone else."

I cannot believe how frequently I have spoken to successful artists, band managers, or even just friends and family who have lost valuable records in either a fire or the more common record-damaging culprit, water damage from a flood. If you live in an area where storms such as hurricanes or tornadoes occur, do not forget to include your records in your insurance policy. Luckily, insuring a record collection can be accomplished the same way you would insure any of the contents in your home.

Understand Your Insurance Policy

You may already have a home insurance policy, but it may not include any or the total value of your record collection. The first course of action would be to figure out the answers to the following questions, which can be done by calling your current insurance provider:

1. Are only valuable items such as jewelry or other valuables covered or are personal articles included? (Vinyl records may be lumped under personal articles and not classified as a valuable item.)
2. Are vinyl records insured under your current policy?
3. What is the total value of contents that are insured under your policy? Once you obtain this information, calculate the value of your record collection along with all the other items you would be required to replace in the case of any instances your insurance covers (which may or may not include fire, flood, robbery, or an act of god).

Once you have these answers, you'll know better which steps to take next. Most likely, you're going to want to document your vinyl collection to prove its existence and value to your insurance company.

How to Document Your Collection for an Insurance Policy

While the bulk of your possessions may be fairly straightforward to replace with insurance funds, you may not be able to find rare records right away, if at all. If you do manage to find them, they may cost much more than you initially purchased them for. To get an accurate measure of how much it would cost to replace your collection, perform an "appraisal" and provide this to your insurance company. Providing documentation of exactly what you possess and the appraised value will furnish the best possibility of insuring your records for the appropriate amount. Here is how to document your record collection:

1. Log in and list your collection on Discogs! You can enter a list of the albums you own into the site. Once you enter your collection, you can select the "Text with Stats" view on the top right-hand corner (it appears as an image of a graph). This will bring you to a view that shows you your entire collection with the minimum, median, and maximum price range listed beside each album. At the top of this page, a minimum, median, and maximum price range for your entire collection is provided. These numbers can help you gauge if it would be worth insuring your collection or not. If the value of your records is lower than what it would cost you to insure your collection, it may not be time for you to invest in insurance.

2. List only one price per each album in your collection. You don't want to list all three prices, because this can cause confusion and potentially enable an insurance company to value your records at the lowest price. When selecting a price, consider the condition of your album. Mint condition records will be valued closer to the maximum value, and damaged records will be valued closer to the minimum price.

3. With your extra-valuable records, check various sources for an assessment on the value of those records, just to be confident you are insured for enough to re-

place the records. Other reputable sources to check include:

- Popsike.com: Allows you to search certain records and access data on how much they have been sold for on eBay, the primary online auction house for records.
- Price guides: There are various published books that offer record-pricing guides; these can be purchased at any bookstore or online on sites such as Amazon.
- Recordmaster.com: An online price guide that charges a nominal fee for using their pricing service.

4. The insurance company will appreciate it if you have multiple sources to validate the amount you are assigning each record. For example, if you list the Discogs median price, note a link to that product directly within your spreadsheet.

5. Submit your documented collection to your insurance company and ask if your policy covers that value. If not, ask the insurance company how to add it to your home policy.

On the annual anniversary of the policy, be sure to update your spreadsheet and provide your insurance provider with the updated value of your collection.

CHAPTER 9

Cleaning and Repairing Records

P roperly cleaning your records will not only increase their longevity, but it will also help to avoid or troubleshoot playback issues. On occasion, you might run into clicks and pops while playing a newly manufactured record—something you can easily fix by cleaning the record. Both new and used records need cleaning in order to achieve the best sound possible. Not to mention, developing proficient cleaning skills will allow you to pick up used records that can be gems if cleaning is all they require.

Always Start with a Clean Record

Whether your records are new or used, they should always be cleaned before being played on a turntable. You'd want to clean a used record for obvious reasons, such as dirt, dust, and any other contaminants it has been exposed to. New records also require cleaning, because they too are often exposed to dirt and dust and can frequently retain a residue from the manufacturing process that is not always visible to the eye.

Records also require cleaning prior to and after playing. When you store a record it still is exposed to dust and dirt. When you play a record, it gets dirty. No matter what sort of contaminant is on your record and why, it can cause pops, clicks, and an unpleasant listening experience.

Very dirty records can be challenging to clean. However, once you clean the record, if you control its cleanliness through the following maintenance methods, it is fairly effortless to manage keeping them clean. When you buy a record, it is best to perform an extensive wet cleaning. Following a thorough wet cleaning, you can use a dry-brush method for maintenance, typically completed before and after playing a record.

BEWARE INTERNET REMEDIES!
Searching online for record-cleaning methods will yield results advising you to clean your records with homemade solutions varying from just water to adding dish soap, alcohol, and other chemicals commonly found in your home. Avoid all of these methods if your goal is to properly preserve your record for a long time.

There are two basic methods for cleaning records:

1. Wet cleaning, typically involving a fluid and a brush or record-cleaning machine
2. Dry cleaning, which involves using a dry brush

Numerous fluids, brushes, and machines are available within all price ranges. Following are a variety of reputable brands along with different methods for cleaning vinyl records.

Wet Cleaning

All recently acquired records, whether new or used, should be cleaned prior to playing using a wet-cleaning method. Wet cleaning a record is done either using a vacuum cleaning machine or a combination of a cleaning solution and a record-cleaning brush. Remember, when choosing a brush and fluid, confirm that they are suitable for the types of materials you are cleaning. Not all fluids and brushes are suitable for shellac records, and certain brushes are not suitable for vinyl records.

There are various methods to cleaning a record, which can primarily be broken down into:

1. One-step cleaning process, using one cleaner to clean the record
2. Two-step cleaning method, which involves two steps of cleaning the record
3. Three-step cleaning

Two- or even three-step cleaning processes are best done using a vacuum cleaner and are effective for exceedingly problematic contaminants such as cigarette smoke, mold, and mildew. The methods and options for cleaning records are endless and a bit overwhelming. I've narrowed down the list to tried-and-true methods and products that are simple and effective.

SKIP THE ALCOHOL

Do not clean shellac records with alcohol products ever! Alcohol will dissolve the shellac compound, permanently damaging your record. Many commercial record cleaners contain alcohol, so when purchasing a cleaner, use only ones you can verify do not contain alcohol.

One-Step Method: Cleaning Brush and Fluid

Although each manufacturer will have specific instructions on how to use its product, here are the general steps performed in a one-step cleaning method using a brush and fluid:

1. Place the record on a flat surface. Detail-oriented collectors prefer to place the record on a cork or rubber turntable mat with a towel or other absorbent cloth underneath it. If you do not own a turntable mat, make sure that whatever surface you choose to place the record on will not damage the record.
2. If available, carefully remove any loose dust with a compressed air can.
3. Apply the fluid to the record or brush, whichever the manufacturer advises.
4. Spread the fluid carefully onto the record with the brush.

5. Brush the record. The direction you should brush the record and the amount of pressure to apply, typically gentle, will be specified by the manufacturer of the fluid you're using.
6. When done brushing, allow the record to completely dry before playing it.

Two- and Three-Step Cleaning Methods

When buying used records, you may encounter tough-to-clean records, such as those that are left smelling like cigarette smoke. In these instances, using a two- or three-step cleaning method may help clear up these types of issues. Two- and three-step methods are essentially the same as the one-step method, just done two or three times using a different cleaning solution each time. Each solution will address specific contaminants, assuring a thorough cleaning.

If you buy records that require using a two- or three-step method, check out the Audio Intelligent website (www.audiointelligent.com/products.htm). The site provides comprehensive details on how to perform two- and three-step methods. Depending on the degree of dirtiness, Audio Intelligent's two- and three-step methods always use an enzymatic-based formula for the first step. This helps loosen and dissolve a variety of contaminants. The second step utilizes their Super Clean Formula solution, which targets contaminants that were not removed by the enzymatic formula. Audio Intelligent also sells an ultra-pure water that has been deionized and is lab-grade quality, which is best suited for cleaning records.

Cleaning Brushes and Recommended Fluids

A cost-effective way to properly clean a record is to use record-cleaning fluid, also called RCF, and an appropriate record-cleaning brush that is suitable for wet cleaning. When choosing a record-cleaning fluid, select one that is manufactured and developed in a laboratory with lab-grade materials and purified water. If water is not purified, it can contain various minerals and other contaminants that can be harmful to your records. If you purchase fluid that needs to be diluted or requires water for record cleaning at any point, use deionized or distilled water to avoid any potential damage. When cleaning your records with a fluid and brush as opposed to a vacuum-cleaning method, it is best to purchase fluids that do not require rinsing, because rinsing a record without a vacuum-cleaning machine can be risky if you're not experienced. Here are particular record-cleaning fluid-and-brush combinations I recommend:

AUDIO INTELLIGENT PREMIUM ONE-STEP FORMULA NO. 6 ($29) WITH LISTENER SELECT 12" BRUSH ($35)
www.audiointelligent.com/products.htm

Audio Intelligent fluids are enzyme based and are manufactured using only lab-grade water that is distilled six times at their laboratory. The Premium One-Step Formula No. 6 is a no-rinse method that requires you to simply apply the fluid to the record surface with a Listener Select or flat-bottom brush, such as the Disc Doctor's brush discussed next, to spread the fluid across the record. Next you gently apply a slight pressure of the brush to the record surface and continue to clean this for 1–3 minutes, allowing the enzymes to loosen and dissolve any contaminants on the record.

THE DISC DOCTOR'S QUICKWASH RECORD CLEANER ($27) WITH THE DISC DOCTOR'S MIRACLE RECORD BRUSH SIZE A ($23.50)
www.discdoc.com

The Disc Doctor's line of brushes are suitable for all types of records including vinyl, shellac, lacquer, and Edison Diamond Discs. The Disc Doctor's flat-bottom brush is particularly good. When combined with the QuickWash Record Cleaner (a blend of purified water and biodegradable surfactants), it is an affordable, highly effective, and simple way to manually clean your records. The QuickWash fluid, which also requires no rinse, is applied to the record by first dispersing the solution onto your brush and using it to gently spread the fluid to the grooved area. It is a remarkably effective and inexpensive way to clean your records.

LAST ALL-PURPOSE RECORD CLEANER ($27)
www.thelastfactory.com

The Last All-Purpose Record Cleaner includes a 2-ounce bottle of fluid and two microfiber applicators. This product is specifically devised to remove residues and contaminants left over from the manufacturing process in addition to everyday dirt, making it an excellent cleaner for newly manufactured records. Last products are simple to use. You apply a designated number of drops to the included applicator and sweep it along the record, following the grooves. It collects dust particles and other residue directly onto the applicator. You can also purchase applicators separately as needed.

Record-Cleaning Machines

Purchasing a vacuum record-cleaning machine, occasionally referred to as a RCM, is the best way to be confident your records are 100 percent clean. There are several record -cleaning systems available on the market. If you are investing in a cleaning machine, choose one with a vacuum. When using a vacuum system, the dirt is suctioned off the record—not being pushed into the grooves—providing you with a completely clean record.

Vacuum record-cleaning machines can be costly, although they will last an extremely long time. If purchasing one is not an option, you may also check your local record store or local electronics dealers because they might own a high-quality record-cleaning machine and charge patrons a small fee to clean records on it. Here are a few vacuum-type record cleaners I recommend:

PRO-JECT VC-S ($449)

Turntable manufacturer Pro-Ject makes a reasonably priced vacuum record cleaner. The machine is strikingly simple to operate. You place the record you wish to clean onto the platter, turn on the machine to start the platter spinning, and while the record spins you add the fluid. You then spread the fluid evenly across the record with a Pro-Ject goat-hair brush. You lower the vacuum arm to the record and turn on the vacuum. If you intend to purchase lots of used records, this is an exceptional record-cleaning machine at the lowest end of the price range.

NITTY GRITTY ($485–$1,459)

Nitty Gritty has been producing high-quality vacuum record-cleaning machines since the 1980s. The current models of Nitty Gritty machines are available within a variety of price ranges.

Their entry-level machine, the Model 1.0, costs $485, the Model 2.0 is $555, and the 30th Anniversary is $630, and all feature manual operations. You manually apply the fluid to the record on the machine with a brush and manually rotate the platter while the machine vacuums.

As you move up in price range to the Nitty Gritty 1.5 and 2.5, the record is automatically rotated during the vacuum cycle. To move up to this feature, this will run you $775–$924. The Fi Model, which costs approximately $1,000, is completely automatic; however, the record needs to be manually turned over to complete cleaning of both sides.

Nitty Gritty also offers two other models. The 2.5Fi-XP is approximately $1,200 and is best utilized for the two-step cleaning method because it can dispense two different fluids interchangeably. The top-of-the-line Nitty Gritty is called the Mini-Pro. It's fully automatic and cleans both sides of the record at one time. The Mini-Pro 1 ($1,379) is housed in a black woodgrain cabinet, and the Mini-Pro 2 ($1,459) is housed in a cherry finish, solid oak cabinet.

CLEARAUDIO ($1,599–$5,499)

Clearaudio offers two record-cleaning machines for the high-end audiophile who wants to ensure the utmost sound quality and preservation of their records. The Smart Matrix Professional, which cleans each record side individually, requires manual application of the fluid to the record. The Double Matrix Professional Sound provides 100 percent automatic application or the ability to control any element of the cleaning process using a control panel. In addition to how efficiently it cleans the records, benefits include the ability to adjust the platter spinning direction while cleaning, which ensures clean grooves, and it is significantly less noisy compared to competing record-cleaning machines.

VPI ($649–$1,200)

Currently, VPI produces two record-cleaning machines—the HW-16.5, a manual machine that costs $649, and the MW-1 Cyclone, which costs approximately $1,200. The HW-16.5 has been in production for more than thirty years and is a reliable, award-winning system. The MW-1 provides you the ability to clean the record both clockwise and counterclockwise, providing a thorough cleaning of the record groove not comparable to other machines.

SPIN-CLEAN RECORD WASHER MKII ($71)

In addition to vacuum cleaners, there is one other record-cleaning device on the market that is used to clean records, the Spin-Clean Record Washer MKII. The Spin-Clean is a simple machine to operate that acts sort of as a bath for your records. You fill the bottom of the machine with a record-cleaning solution and distilled or deionized water and spin your record through the bath. If you buy a large collection of really dirty old records, the Spin-Clean is a cost-effective way to perform an initial wet cleaning. However, after you run the records through the Spin-Clean, I advise that you perform a second wet cleaning using a brush-and-fluid combination to make sure the records are thoroughly cleaned.

Dry Cleaning

Dry brushes are utilized to maintain record cleanliness. I recommend using a dry brush before and after playing a record that has been cleaned recently either with a cleaning machine or the liquid-and-brush method previously mentioned.

The type of brush you use depends on the type of record you are playing. When cleaning a polyvinyl "vinyl" record, use a carbon fiber brush. Carbon fiber is strong enough to clear away dirt and soft enough to not cause scratches within the grooves. Using a carbon fiber brush also aids in the removal of static, making it an ideal cleaning tool to use before playing the record. There are countless companies out there that are making dry brushes. Here are the dry brushes that I highly recommend:

- AcousTech Anti-Static Record Brush: $20
- Audioquest Anti-Static Record Cleaner: $15
- Hunt EDA Mark 6 Brush: $30

INNER-GROOVE DISTORTION
Songs that are closer to the center label on a record have audible differences over those on the outer edge. The audio within the ridge and valleys of the grooves that are closer to the center label start to become closer together, which can affect the needle's ability to track accurately. Be sure to keep that area clean.

To clean shellac, acetates, or Edison Diamond Discs with a dry brush, you need to purchase a brush that is specifically recommended for cleaning these materials, such as The Disc Doctor's Miracle Record Brush Size D.

Antistatic Record Guns

The Milty Zerostat 3 is an antistatic gun that removes static charges from your records. You point it at the record from approximately 2–6 inches away, pull the trigger, and slowly release it. The Zerostat 3 is estimated to last for around 10,000 pulls and costs approximately $100. Once you remove the static from the record, the record will collect less dust and other particles. In addition to records, the gun can be used on film, glass, CDs, DVDs, and lenses.

Record-Cleaning Methods to Avoid

A simple search on Google on how to clean a record will yield endless horrible options for cleaning a record. If you are investing effort into cleaning a record, pick up a brush and the fluid I recommend and avoid the risk of damaging your records and turntable.

Wood Glue

A few years ago, coinciding with the start of media reports regarding the vinyl boom, a video on YouTube shared a method of cleaning your records using wood glue. In no time the video went viral, boasting over 1.6 million views! Essentially, glue is applied to the grooved area of a spinning record. The glue-covered record is set aside to dry overnight. When dry, the glue is manually peeled off, producing a smooth and clean record.

It seems like a good idea, but I do not recommend this method. It is time-consuming and if you are not patient when removing the glue, you can damage the record. Not to mention, the video advises you to apply glue to a record while it is on your turntable and to smooth it out without getting any on the center label, two actions that seem too risky for my liking.

Dish Soap

Cleaning vinyl records with dish soap is a common practice. If you elect to experiment with this method, bear in mind that commercial products and soap compositions are modified over the years and vary from brand to brand. If you can't determine exactly what chemicals are in your soap and how vinyl will react to them, it is best to avoid. Another reason to avoid this method is because it is commonly used with tap water and a cloth that may scratch your record. If you possess a fairly cheap record you are not too concerned with damaging and you experiment with this method, be sure to mix with distilled water and use a record brush or cloth that will not scratch the record.

REMEMBER, IT'S ALL FOR FUN
Practicing all the cleaning, storage, and protection methods explained in this chapter will keep you confidently collecting records and preserving your music for many years of enjoyment. Even though I share some really meticulous details on how to care for your collection, don't feel too overwhelmed. Not every record or record collection requires fastidious cleaning and care.

Record-Cleaning Fluids to Avoid

There are many record-cleaning products on the market that you should avoid. When it comes to buying record-cleaning solutions, avoid the ones that provide you little to no information on the ingredients used to concoct their solution. If they do not provide you with information on what you are using, it is unlikely beneficial for your records, and in certain instances it can be detrimental. If you come across a cleaning fluid not mentioned in this book, do a bit of research and find reviews written by reputable record collectors before committing to it or using it on valuable records.

How to Fix a Warped Record

Despite your best efforts to maintain your records, sometimes one will warp. Or, you'll buy one that's warped because it's a great find. There are two things you need to flatten a warped record: heat and heavy objects to sandwich the record between. Many websites advise using a stove at a very low temperature, but I am hesitant to try this, let alone advise it.

I gather all my warped records together and wait until the warm summer months. I then sandwich each album between two heavy books and put the stack into a room that hits warm temperatures (approximately 85°F–90°F). I leave them there for at least a week, longer if possible, and most of the time the records become unwarped—or at least much less warped and in more of a playable condition.

Fixing Scratches on Records

Although there are many resources claiming that you can fix scratches on a record with sandpaper, ice, and so on, I've never been able to make those ideas work. I have, however, had success reducing the noise from scratches and needle drops by using a wet melamine foam brush (Magic Eraser). (Don't try this on a record you are too concerned with losing if this does not work for you.) To try, follow these steps:

1. Thoroughly clean a record using a proper cleaning method such as a two- or three-step method first.

2. Use deionized or distilled water to wet the melamine
   foam brush. Squeeze out excess water.
3. Lightly scrub the scratch or needle-drop damage
   with the brush.

This method doesn't always work and is by no means a miracle cure, but it has helped me several times and should only be tried after using all proper cleaning methods.

One other thing I noticed about noises caused by scratches is that on occasion, after playing the album a few times, the noise from the scratch can reduce itself on its own and be less noticeable. Regardless, if you are going to purchase many used records, the occasional scratch that causes a second or two of imperfection on an album shouldn't matter that much.

CHAPTER 10

More Advanced Collecting: First Pressings, Reissues, and Other Special Pressings

*W*ith everything you have learned up to this point in the book, you are now equipped to head out there and begin building the ultimate vinyl collection. What sort of collector are you? Are you in search of rare titles in pristine condition that are or will be of value in the years to come? Are you searching for impeccable pressings that offer an audiophile experience? Or are you simply trying to find decent recordings from your favorite artists? Will you collect records for specific artists or labels only? Are you interested in finding antique records, maybe shellacs or cylinders? Whatever category of records you decide to hunt, various tools are provided throughout this chapter to ease the process of finding those records.

You'll Find So Many Records to Choose From!

Today's typical music enthusiasts aren't seeking out just the current hits—they possess a passion for music across a variety of genres, spanning over various decades. This means that chasing after a certain title that is not a recent release may be difficult. Consider also that the title you want may not be readily available in new condition or that several pressings of it may be available. If a title is several years old, there are possibly various different pressings for several different countries or regions. Select versions may be released by the artists on their original label. Other pressings may be reissued by a licensing label. Over the years, the record may have also been pressed at different plants, or mastered by different engineers. This can leave a collector confused as to which copy to buy.

You might not even need to buy the highest-valued version of a specific pressing, but, possessing the skills to identify a pressing will save you from overpaying for an album or landing a manufacturing dud. Alongside the media hype of vinyl's resurgence, I have noticed an increasing number of people who attempt to sell secondhand records and expect ten-plus times the actual value of their records. You by no means are required to be a record-appraising expert, but the more informed you are, the better you're able to negotiate confidently.

In this chapter I also introduce you to reissue labels, which are record labels that license and officially release titles from the parent label that owns the rights to the album. Reissue labels are an excellent resource for vinyl for two reasons— they are making available titles that the parent label does not have an interest in releasing on vinyl, and they are releasing higher-quality versions of releases.

Different Pressings of the Same Album

With various pressings available for a single release, it can become very difficult to understand what pressing you have or are looking at. You may listen to a 1970 copy of *Led Zeppelin III* at a friend's house, then eventually score an exceptional copy of *Led Zeppelin III* for yourself . . . but find out it does not sound the same as your friend's copy. If the album has no scratches, this variance is probably due to the fact that the pressing you acquired is inferior in comparison to your friend's.

There are many reasons that the same album can sound or look different:

- Frequently, albums are mastered or remastered by different engineers.
- Records are often pressed at multiple pressing plants, which can create differences in the quality of the LPs.
- The print materials included, such as the center label, album, insert, poster, or other bonus items, may be different in each pressing. .

These differences create both opportunities and difficulties for collectors. Regardless, all the available pressings of the same album means more vinyl to track down for vinyl hunters.

Catalog Number

Each release is assigned a catalog number, which is a number or a number-letter combination appointed by the record label. Prior to the widespread practice of implementing UPC barcodes for vinyl releases, catalog numbers were the clearest identifying number for titles. Different pressings can have different catalog numbers. A catalog number can change based on territory, meaning that a release in the United States will have a different catalog number than one in Australia. Once UPC barcodes were introduced, the majority of catalog numbers were replaced with UPCs.

Finding the catalog number is the first way to identify what release you possess, but it is only a starting point. You can locate the catalog number by checking the center labels of a record, the jacket, and the etched matrix of an album. Once you locate the catalog number, you can easily locate detailed pressing information pertaining to the release through Discogs. Continuing with the *Led Zeppelin III* album example, a search of its catalog number (SD 7201) on Discogs yielded 102 results! Here is how to narrow down these results.

Release Year and Country

The results I found through Discogs show various pressings over a number of years, ranging from the 1970s through the 1990s, with numerous countries it was released in. From here, you can attempt to narrow it down by locating the release year and country on the album you have. This is usually printed somewhere on the release, typically on the jacket, center label, or on any other printed material.

Matrix and Other Identifiers

Albums predating the 1980s did not often contain barcodes and instead featured a catalog number and other identifiers. These identifiers were either inscribed or machine-stamped onto the dead wax area of a record or noted on the center label of an album. This identifier is referred to during the manufacturing process to assist in keeping track of the release. The matrix number on an album can tell collectors a story. The numbers and letters within the markings can possibly include the catalog number, a master engineer number that indicates who mastered the album or created the lacquers, and a plant identifier indicating at what pressing plant the record was produced.

Back to the *Led Zeppelin III* release. Due to its commercial success upon the album's initial release, *Led Zeppelin III* was pressed by various pressing plants throughout the world, in addition to multiple plants within the United States, in order to satisfy release-date demands. Here are just a few examples of the matrix identifier for the 1970 *Led Zeppelin III* U.S. pressings that were pressed at various pressing plants:

- **Matrix/runout on side A center label:** ST-A-702005-B MO and side B: ST-A-702006-A MO—The "MO" at the end of the number indicates this version was pressed at Monarch Record Mfg. Co., which was a record-pressing facility in Los Angeles, California.
- **Matrix/runout on side A center label:** ST-A-702005-B PR and side B: ST-A-702006-A PR—The "PR" at the end of this number indicates this version was pressed at Presswell, which was a pressing plant located in Ancora, New Jersey.

- **Matrix/runout on side A center label:** ST-A-702005 RI and side B: ST-A-702006 RI—The "RI" at the end of the matrix indicates this was an Atlantic release pressed at the Philips Recording Company in Richmond, Indiana.

The engineer who creates the lacquers also often inscribes in the matrix some kind of signifying indicator. For example, Stan Ricker, a famous vinyl engineer who was the leader in half-speed mastering, etched SR/2 or SR2 on albums he mastered.

For the *Led Zeppelin III* example, here is an example of a dead-wax etching that indicates information for the mastering house that created the lacquers for this pressing:

- **Matrix/runout (side two):** ST A 702006 - E-4EE I-IIII (2) TWO Mastercraft—The "Mastercraft" indicates that the lacquers for this release were created at Mastercraft.

HIDDEN MESSAGES ON THE MATRIX

In addition to numbers and letters that identify something specific about how the record was manufactured, artists or engineers have also included hidden messages or phrases on the matrix. These hidden messages are not always available on all pressings, making them more valuable over other pressings.

The very first UK pressing of Elvis Costello's 1978 release *This Year's Model* had "Special pressing No. 003 Ring Moira on 434 3232 for your special prize" etched into the matrix. The first people, estimated to be around a thousand, who called that phone number received a photo with a printed autograph and a badge that stated "Made in 1955 for 1984."

There are hundreds, maybe even thousands, of different matrix markings that represent a record-pressing plant, engineer, or mastering house. A comprehensive list, providing a number of detailed matrix examples and their meanings, was created by a Discogs member. Visit this link: www .discogs.com/help/forums/topic/221240.

Artwork Identifiers

The album artwork itself is another valuable indicator of what pressing you have or are in search of.

MISPRINTS
When creating album art, sometimes a misprint or typo slips through but is fixed for later pressings. Misprints can include anything from a typo, misspelled word, not listing a song, ordering the tracking listing incorrectly, and other errors. On occasion, these artist blunders create copies that are highly sought after because the misprint version is scarce.

PACKAGING
Not all packaging is created equal! Some artwork is purposely designed differently across various pressings. Occasionally, limited packaging designs are created for select markets, for the initial release only, for artist fan clubs, and various other special reasons. By the 1970s, labels frequently experimented with different record colors and releasing limited-edition picture discs.

Back to the *Led Zeppelin III* example. Several versions of the original pressings within the United States, Canada, the United Kingdom, and a few other European countries were released with a gatefold jacket that included a rotating pinwheel. The cover of the France version was completely different and included a flipback cover, which is a cover that is held together with flaps that fold to the back of the cover from the front. A version found in Uruguay features the image of the wheel as a cover. Various other territories had slightly different covers, with several not including the wheel at all. Examining and identifying unique packaging can help you determine a specific pressing.

What Pressing Do You Have? A Step-by-Step ID Process

Now that you understand the numerous ways to identify unique markings, here is a simple way to use those clues to determine further details relevant to your record:

1. Collect as much information as possible about the pressing, such as catalog numbers, matrix markings, and special artwork details.
2. Search this information at Discogs to figure out and verify the exact details on this pressing. Discogs often has thorough information on each pressing that will likely provide you a lot of insight and enlightening details on your record.
3. Perform a search on the Steve Hoffman Music Forums: www.forums.stevehoffman.tv/.

The Steve Hoffman Music Forums are an online community of more than 50,000 vinyl collectors. The members of the forums are genuinely knowledgeable and are often longtime collectors. This is an excellent resource not only for assisting with verifying certain pressing details but to also connect with some knowledgeable people who can provide you with insight on various pressings. If you have performed extensive research and are still stuck figuring out specifics of a pressing, sign up for the Steve Hoffman forum and seek the knowledge of other members.

Original and First Pressings

Quite often you will hear collectors mention they are in search of an "original" or "first pressing" of a certain album. The terms "first pressing," "first press," "first issue," "original press," or "original issue" are used interchangeably in reference to the earlier pressing of an album, but they actually each bear slightly different and specific definitions.

- **First pressing/ first issue:** This is the very first pressing of an album ever made.
- **Original pressing/original issue:** This means it is an original pressing, not a reissue.

There are two situations that create confusion and difficulty in identifying first and original pressings.

1. The first is that these two terms are loosely referred to and there is no real definitive interpretation to them. When purchasing an album that is claimed to be a first pressing, use all the information available to you (catalog number, matrix etchings, etc.) to be sure you know what you're getting. Sellers aren't always correct about the pressing they possess, and on rare occasions some sellers are directly misleading.
2. The second is that for large releases, both the first and original pressings can be done at various plants using different record stampers, which often means the records have different markings on the matrix of

the record. An excellent example of this is The Beatles's self-titled album, often referred to as *The White Album*. If you locate and view the album on Discogs, you will come across more than twenty different variations of this album from the year it was originally released. The majority of them have different catalog numbers on the jacket and were pressed in different regions. This makes defining what is considered the "first" pressing and what is the "original" pressing a bit difficult. Discogs is an excellent resource for figuring out first and original pressings for the majority of releases.

Don't forget: Discogs will also provide you with an estimated amount this album sells for regardless of what pressing it is, so you can be sure you are buying it at an appropriate price point.

MOST VALUABLE RECORD EVER SOLD

The Beatles *The White Album*, released in 1968, is the most valuable record of all time, with Ringo Starr auctioning off his personal copy of the mono UK version for $790,000 in 2015! Prior to that, a low-numbered first pressing with serial number 0000005 sold for $30,000. With news reports of these insanely expensive auctions, people understandably think that all first pressings of *The White Album* are extremely valuable. However, there were so many "original pressings" made throughout 1968 that the release is actually readily available and not excessively overpriced. The lion's share of valuable versions are the UK mono first pressings, recognizable by the EMI text missing on the center label. That particular version can fetch hundreds of dollars when in excellent condition.

Vinyl Reissues

A reissue is the rerelease of an album that has already been out before. A reissue usually has some sort of addition or alteration to set it apart from the original release. The difference may be within the artwork, such as a different center label, cover, or an additional poster or insert. Many are quick to jump to the conclusion that reissues are of lesser quality or value than the original, although that is frequently far from the truth. Sometimes, reissues come years after the original album was released and are remastered by a top-notch engineer to sound phenomenal in comparison to its predecessors.

In other instances, particularly releases from the 1990s to the present, vinyl reissues were created using a retail CD or retail digital source as opposed to the original source, making for a record with horrible sound quality. The unfortunate reality is that from time to time, a CD or a retail digital version is the only master source available. There is a general understanding among collectors that if a record was mastered from a retail CD or retail digital source, it's not a great vinyl option.

Some albums mastered from retail CD or digital sources are actually good—and that's because they were properly mastered for vinyl and the lacquers were cut by a reputable engineer, who applies mastering skills to assure they sound top-notch. The CD-to-vinyl process usually fabricates terrible-sounding records due to the fact that the lacquer is created by an employee in a mastering house who is not a skilled, professional lacquer-cutting engineer.

On the other side of the spectrum, you could have an incredible master source file, yet if you do not enlist a quality engineer, you can still end up with a horrible vinyl product. If you want to acquire the best-sounding pressing of a title, the paramount option would be a pressing that employed the best sources available (hopefully not CD or low-quality digital files), mastered and cut for vinyl by a professional vinyl engineer.

Vinyl Reissues from Record Labels

You might encounter a vinyl version of a title released by a different label than the original. These are typically referred to as reissue labels. Reissue record labels have existed for several decades and should be credited in a large way for keeping vinyl alive. Reissue labels often release a title:

- That has been out of print for a long time and is only available, if even available at all, in a used condition;
- With art and or music at a higher quality than what is currently available;
- That has never been in the vinyl format.

If your goal is to acquire high-quality pressings, definitely check out reissue labels, because a lot of the titles they release are of the highest quality. In addition to reissue labels, there are several vinyl-only labels that release and reissue titles on vinyl and are often recognized for their uniqueness, high-quality audio and artwork, and limited availability. Following are a variety of vinyl-passionate reissue labels I highly recommend checking out.

Analogue Productions

Analogue Productions is a vinyl-reissue label founded by Chad Kassem, who also founded the online vinyl store

Acoustic Sounds. Analogue Productions primarily releases jazz, blues, rock, folk, and classical albums on vinyl, CDs, and Super Audio CDs (SACDs), which are CDs that can offer more channels, such as surround sound, and longer playing time than a regular CD. Kassem launched Analogue Productions in 1992 with the goal of offering albums he enjoyed on vinyl. In 1994, Chad purchased a 1920s Gothic-style church, which became Blue Heaven Studios, a recording studio where all Analogue Productions Originals (APO) releases are recorded. In 2011, Chad opened Quality Record Pressings (QRP), a vinyl-pressing plant that incorporates innovations to improve the record-pressing process, further improving the quality of the Analogue Productions product. Although the pressing plant is barely five years old, it has gained a reputation for releasing a number of the highest-quality reissues on the market. All Analogue Productions releases are pressed by QRP in addition to several other titles available through various record labels. If you come across a QRP pressing, you can be confident you will be purchasing a high-quality release that was pressed with care and precision.

Catalog Highlights
- First record released: Virgil Thomson *The Plow That Broke the Plains/Suite from "The River"* LP
- Hard to find: Bill Evans *Riverside Recordings* 22 LP box set (median Discogs price: $1,052)

My Top Five:
- Norah Jones *Not Too Late* LP
- Cat Stevens *Tea for the Tillerman* LP
- The Doors *Morrison Hotel* LP
- Vince Guaraldi Trio *A Charlie Brown Christmas* LP
- Nina Simone *Little Girl Blue* LP

Friday Music

Established by Joe Reagoso in 2002, Friday Music specializes in reissues of various rock, pop, blues, R&B, and jazz releases on both CD and vinyl. Prior to starting Friday Music, Joe worked in radio promotions, enabling him to build relationships with all the major labels and with a number of their artists. Many of the artists Joe worked with became friends and are now on the Friday Music label. Key titles range from artists including the Monkees, David Bowie, Elvis, Chicago, Boston, and more.

Catalog Highlights
- First record released: Flash *Flash* CD
- Hard to find: The Grateful Dead *Live at the Cow Palace, New Year's Eve 1976* 5XLP (median Discogs price: $105)

My Top Five
- Sugarhill Gang *Rapper's Delight: The Best of Sugarhill Gang* 2XLP
- Various Artists *The Lost Boys Original Motion Picture Soundtrack* LP
- David Bowie *Heathen* LP
- David Bowie *A Reality Tour* 3XLP
- Santana *Lotus* 3XLP

Legacy Recordings

Sony Music established Legacy Recordings in 1990 to archive and preserve their extensive catalog, with various titles over 100 years old. Shortly after its inception, Legacy

Recordings began to release various Sony reissues on the Legacy imprint. Sony is diligent in preserving and archiving its catalog, enabling Legacy to access quality sources for its reissues.

Catalog Highlights
- First record released: First releases were primarily CDs with the first vinyl title likely Slug the Nightwatchman *Slug the Nightwatchman* LP
- Hard to find: Pearl Jam *1990–1992 Boxed Set Sampler* (sold for $1,000 on eBay in 2014; median Discogs price: $300)

My Top Five
- Foo Fighters *In Your Honor* 2XLP
- Dave Matthews Band *Crash* 2XLP
- Pearl Jam *Ten* LP
- Fugees *The Score* LP
- Modest Mouse *The Moon & Antarctica* 2XLP

Light in the Attic Records

Light in the Attic Records is a Seattle-based label and concert production company established in 2002 by Matt Sullivan. Matt began his career interning for labels such as Sub Pop and eventually launched Light in the Attic to accommodate his desire for reissuing vinyl. Over the years Light in the Attic has reissued titles on vinyl from artists such as The Last Poets, The Black Angels, Betty Davis, Kris Kristofferson, and more. Light in the Attic also has two imprint labels with the first, Cinewax, recognized for releasing soundtracks such as *Shogun Assassin* and *Jodorowsky's*

Dune on limited vinyl. Their second imprint, Modern Classic Recordings, was launched in 2011 and has released titles such as Willie Nelson *Teatro*, Built to Spill *Ultimate Alternative Wavers*, and The Stone Roses *The Stone Roses*.

Catalog Highlights
- First record released: The Last Poets *The Last Poets/ This Is Madness* LP
- Hard to find: Mark Lanegan *Has God Seen My Shadow? An Anthology 1989–2011* 3XLP (median Discogs price: $64)

My Top Five
- Heartworn Highways *40th Anniversary* 2LP wooden box set
- The Black Angels *Passover* 2XLP
- This Heat *Deceit* LP
- Rodriguez *Searching for Sugar Man Original Motion Picture Soundtrack* LP
- Epic Soundtracks *Rise Above* LP

Mobile Fidelity Sound Lab

With roughly forty years in business, Mobile Fidelity Sound Lab's (often referred to as MFSL or MoFi) releases are still recognized for their high-fidelity sound. Although MoFi officially began in 1977, you will find a few releases, primarily recordings of steam engines, that predate 1977 and are attributed as Mobile Fidelity Records releases. Founder Brad Miller was a producer and recording engineer who recorded the outdoor environment and man-made machine sounds.

The first four Mobile Fidelity Sound Lab releases were by Mystic Moods Orchestra, which was an experimental pop group created by Brad Miller. Following these releases the subsequent five MFSL releases included Supertramp *Crime of the Century*, John Klemmer *Touch*, Steely Dan *Katy Lied*, Los Angeles Philharmonic Orchestra *Zubin Mehta Conducts Suites from John Williams' Star Wars and Close Encounters of the Third Kind*, and Al Stewart *Year of the Cat*. By the end of the 1970s, MFSL were reissuing titles from artists such as Pink Floyd, The Grateful Dead, Fleetwood Mac, and other notable artists and albums from that era. Although vinyl sales were close to obsolete by the 1990s, Mobile Fidelity continued to reissue countless, high-quality titles on vinyl.

Catalog Highlights
- First record released: No Artist *Memories in Steam* LP
- Hard to find: The Rolling Stones *The Rolling Stones* 11XLP (Discogs median price: $850)

My Top Five
- Nirvana *Nevermind* LP
- Sonic Youth *Goo* LP
- Pink Floyd *Atom Heart Mother* LP
- Beck *Sea Change* 2XLP
- Weezer *Weezer (The Blue Album)* LP

Mondo Music

Mondo Music is a division of the pop culture/art company Mondo, that is well-known for creating limited-edition art such as prints, posters, T-shirts, and other collectibles for classic and contemporary films, television shows, and comics.

The music division releases a variety of soundtracks on limited vinyl that include customized artwork created by a series of artists they work with. They often create or hire prominent artists to produce their album art and pair it with a uniquely pressed vinyl record. In addition to vinyl collectors, art, comic book, and movie collectors often hunt for Mondo releases.

Catalog Highlights
- First record released: Jay Chattaway *Maniac* LP
- Hard to find: James Horner *Aliens* (Xenomorph blood liquid-filled record) LP (has sold on eBay for as high as $800)

My Top Five
- Mike Shinoda and Joseph Trapanese *The Raid: Redemption* 2XLP
- Cliff Martinez *Drive* 2XLP
- John Williams *Home Alone* 2XLP
- James Horner *Aliens* (Xenomorph blood liquid-filled record) LP
- Shirley Walker *Superman The Animated Series* 12-inch die-cut record

Rhino Records

Although Rhino Records started in 1973 as a Los Angeles record shop, it transformed into a record label in 1978. Throughout the 1970s and 1980s, Rhino primarily released reissues, compilation albums, and novelty records featuring comedy performers. In 1985, Rhino signed a distribution agreement with Capitol Records that granted them access to reissue selections from the Capitol catalog. In 1992, Rhino signed a distribution deal with Atlantic Records and in turn Time Warner purchased a 50 percent stake in Rhino. In 1998, Time Warner purchased the remaining 50 percent of Rhino. With this merger, Rhino now had access to artists such as The Doors, The Monkees, Doobie Brothers, Ramones, and more. Today, Rhino is a member of the Warner Music Group family and is frequently responsible for the Warner Music vinyl reissues, including The Doors, Led Zeppelin, The Cure, The Smiths, Joy Division, Van Halen, The Velvet Underground, Mike Oldfield, and more.

Catalog Highlights
- First record released: Wild Man Fischer *Wildmania* LP (RNLP 001)
- Hard to find: Third Eye Blind *Third Eye Blind Vinyl Box Set*

My Top Five
- Madonna *Like a Prayer* LP
- The Velvet Underground *Loaded* LP
- Circles Around the Sun *Interludes for the Dead* 2XLP
- Alanis Morissette *Jagged Little Pill* LP
- The Smiths *The Smiths* LP

SRCVinyl

While a large portion of reissue labels primarily deal with titles predating the 1990s, my label, SRCVinyl, primarily releases titles from the 1990s through the present that were either pressed to vinyl or were done so in extremely limited quantities. We launched our reissue division in 2011 with our first release, Mock Orange *Nines & Sixes*. However, Mock

Orange was not intended to be our first release because SRC001 was assigned to Yellowcard *One for the Kids*, which was released about two years later due to the inability to reproduce the cover art and artist sensitivity issues between the band and the original label, Lobster Records. Currently we are reissuing several 90s and early 2000s titles from artists such as the entire Blink-182 catalog and albums from artists such as Silverchair, Alkaline Trio, Gin Blossoms, Sum 41, Our Lady Peace, and Local H.

Catalog Highlights
- First record released: Mock Orange *Nines & Sixes* LP
- Hard to find: Blink-182 *Take Off Your Pants and Jacket* LP plus 3X7-inch (Discogs median price: $138)

My Top Five
- Say Anything *In Defense of the Genre* 2XLP
- Silverchair *Frogstomp* 2XLP
- Blink-182 *Enema of the State* 2XLP
- Various Artists *Forrest Gump* 2XLP
- Teenage Wrist *Dazed* 2XLP

Sundazed Music

Located in Coxsackie, New York, Sundazed Music specializes in releasing obscure and rare albums from the 1950s through the 1970s. Sundazed was founded by Bob Irwin and his wife Mary back in 1989 with the goal to reissue sophisticated-sounding CDs and vinyl. Sundazed Music began after Bob left his job as a record-store manager and started working on music restoration projects. The quality of his work was noticed by the major labels, who enlisted him to reissue various projects on CD and vinyl. Sundazed Music is known for its attention to detail and in-house preproduction mixing and mastering.

Catalog Highlights
- First record released: The Knickerbockers *The Great Lost Knickerbockers Album* LP
- Hard to find: Ben Folds *Ben Folds Live* LP (Discogs median price: $69)

My Top Five
- Bob Dylan *Blonde on Blonde* LP
- Mr. Gasser and the Weirdos *Surfink!* LP
- Johnny Cash *At Folsom Prison* LP
- Hot Tuna *Hot Tuna* LP
- Simon and Garfunkel *Bridge Over Troubled Water* LP

Third Man Records

Found in 2001 by Jack White of The White Stripes, Third Man Records is an independent label originally headquartered in Detroit, Michigan, but now also located in Nashville, Tennessee. Although Third Man releases a part of their catalog digitally and on CD, the label is primarily focused on vinyl releases, curated in a number of cases by Jack White himself. The majority of Third Man Records releases are made available on black vinyl, with colored vinyl predominately only available at their store in Nashville and through their quarterly subscription, the Vault.

Setting Third Man Records apart from other vinyl labels is Jack White's knack for pushing boundaries and creating unique vinyl releases. Innovations include glow-in-the-dark records, a scented record, liquid-filled records, a rose petal–filled record, a playable etched record, an x-ray record, and most recently playing the first record in space. Most of these innovative releases are quite pricey and difficult to locate. The scented record was a peach-scented album pressed for Jack White's former wife Karen Elson and her *The Ghost Who Walks* release. This limited release, when found, will cost you $100–$200. Also for Karen Elson, a limited 7-inch was pressed with rose petals arranged inside the vinyl. This pressing was limited to 1,000 copies and goes for around $75–$100. One of the most valuable Third Man releases was Jack White's "Sixteen Saltines" liquid-filled record, which sold on eBay for $1,336 in 2012. However, this is now available for under $500 with notes from sellers that the liquid has leaked or dried up.

Third Man Records also releases a vinyl series titled Third Man Live, which are full-length albums recorded in the Third Man Blue Room, a concert hall where a band can set up and perform live to an audience while recording the performance to a direct-to-tape setup. The shows are recorded on a 1-inch 8-track tape, then mixed to a 2-track tape that is sourced to cut the vinyl master. Limited-edition split blue and black colored vinyl is made available only to the audience who attend the performance and Vault members on rare occasions. The performances are also made available on an unlimited number of black vinyl variants. Performers have included Jack Johnson, The Shins, The Raconteurs, the Black Lips, Jerry Lee Lewis, Wanda Jackson, and more.

Catalog Highlights

- First record released: The Dead Weather "Hang You from the Heavens/Are 'Friends' Electric?" 7-inch

- Hard to find: The Dead Weather *Blue Blood Blues* 12-inch triple-decker with "I Feel Strange/Rolling in on a Burning Tire" 7-inch embedded within the 12-inch (Discogs median price: $500)

My Top Five
- The White Stripes *Elephant* 2XLP
- Jack White *Lazaretto* LP
- The Black Belles *The Black Belles* LP
- Death from Above 1979 *Live at Third Man Records* LP
- Elvis Presley "My Happiness/That's When Your Heartaches Begin" 10-inch

Waxwork Records

Although a fairly new vinyl-only and reissue label, Waxwork Records has released a large number of horror, cult, and sci-fi scores on limited-edition, high-quality vinyl since their launch in 2013. Waxwork Records releases tend to sell out fairly quickly with the limited versions often only available directly through them on their website: www.waxworkrecords.com.

Catalog Highlights
- First record released: Richard Band *Re-Animator* LP
- Hard to find: Harry Manfredini *Friday the 13th* blood-filled LP (Discogs median price: $675)

My Top Five
- Harry Manfredini *Friday the 13th* LP
- Danny Elfman *Goosebumps* 2XLP
- John Harrison *Creepshow* LP

- Christopher Komeda *Rosemary's Baby* LP
- Various *Tales from the Darkside: The Movie* LP

FIRST RECORD PLAYED IN SPACE
To celebrate their seventh anniversary, Third Man Records along with their electronics consultant Kevin Carrico created the "ICARUS CRAFT," a custom "spaceproof" turntable which they attached to a high-altitude balloon and launched into space on July 2, 2016. While soaring up to a peak altitude of 94,413 feet the turntable continuously played Third Man Records' 3 millionth pressed album, Carl Sagan's *A Glorious Dawn*.

Promotional Records

Promotional records are albums distributed for free by a record label to promote an upcoming album. They are typically provided to club and radio DJs, radio station programmers, journalists, music producers, and other music-industry individuals. Occasionally, promotional records are distributed prior to the release date, and can contain a remixed version not readily available to the public or exclusive to radio play.

Promo records are usually indicated as such with various markings, including:

- The center label and record jacket are marked with "Promo Only" or "For Promotional Use Only" or something similar stamped on it.
- Record jacket has a corner cut off or cut out, deterring retail sale.
- The record jacket may be different than the regular release. It may be a black-and-white version of the art,

or if it is a promotional single, it is often housed in a plain jacket with a sticker indicating what the album is.
- Occasionally the promotional record will include contact information for a marketing or label representative.

Promotional records were produced in very limited pressings in comparison to their retail counterparts, making them frequently of higher value over the retail version. The promotional versions of albums were often pressed before the actual release was pressed, which causes certain collectors to believe that promos can have improved sound over the actual record. (Record stampers used to press records often wear out, causing certain collectors to think that the first records off the press sound superior to the last records off the press.)

IF YOU COLLECT MONO
Despite mono recordings being phased out in the late sixties, frequently labels would still press mono, promotional-only records that they gave to AM radio stations that only broadcasted in mono. Mono recordings sound extremely different from the stereo versions. Acquiring mono promotional records may be the only way to acquire a mono pressing of certain titles, making them desirable among a group of collectors.

One downfall to collecting promo records is that it's very difficult to find them in a decent or even usable condition. If the promo was of a popular album, the records were spun heavily by DJs.

Led Zeppelin Promotional Albums

Led Zeppelin mono promotional pressings are highly sought after by collectors and when found in mint condition can sell for thousands of dollars!

"Babe I'm Gonna Leave You/Dazed & Confused" mono 45 EP
- Sold for $3,000 March 13, 2016
- Sold for $3,052 August 18, 2013

Houses of the Holy mono LP
- Sold for $2,650 December 1, 2015
- Sold for $1,042 February 3, 2010

Led Zeppelin III mono LP
- Sold for $2,269 December 26, 2009
- Sold for $1,425 August 13, 2014
- Sold for $1,410 December 28, 2012

Test Pressings

These are the records that come off the press first, even prior to promotional copies. Test pressings are provided to the record label and are used for quality control to assure the music being pressed off the plates is flawless. Test pressings are rare, with select record labels pressing as few as 3–5 copies, making them extremely valuable. Unlike promotional copies, test pressings are not widely distributed, making them extremely rare to find. Here are some test pressings that have sold for insane amounts of money.

- Sex Pistols "God Save the Queen": Sold for $12,502 on July 15, 2012
- The Beatles *Please Please Me*: Sold for $12,811 on August 8, 2015
- Bob Dylan *Blood on the Tracks*: Sold for $8,000 on August 26, 2010

Valuable Records

What factors make one record more valuable than another? Many people believe all original or first pressings are the most valuable. But what about a version with interesting packaging? Or maybe the version that sounds the best? Simply put, just like any market, records with the highest value are the ones for which the demand exceeds the supply. Therefore, a reissue that was released ten years after the album was originally released, on a different label, with only 500 copies ever pressed, for an artist that warrants tens of thousands in sales, may be the highest-appraised version.

Record Store Day

Record Store Day is the largest record-collectors event, essentially a record collector's Christmas, only in April. The first Record Store Day was April 19, 2008, and it continues to occur annually on the third Saturday of each April. This day is a celebration of the record store, the customer, and the musicians who of course make this music available. Just about every single record store across North America and countless throughout the world offer a giant celebration on this day, which includes official Record Store Day releases, sales, live performances, and other events organized by the record store.

Special Releases

A Record Store Day committee works with various independent and major labels to designate several titles that are sanctioned as official Record Store Day titles and only available through participating stores worldwide. These titles are limited and desired by record collectors to the extent that many begin lining up hours, even days prior to the store opening.

Record Store Day releases are always limited in quantity, and a hefty portion sell out in stores within the first hour. If you are in search of a record, or several records, on the list, you have to head out to your local record shop early that day.

KANYE WEST *THE LIFE OF PABLO* RECORD STORE DAY BOOTLEGS

With the release of his 2016 album *The Life of Pablo*, Kanye swore the release would never be made available in the CD format, and indeed, he never ended up releasing his new album officially in any physical format. However, just in time for Record Store Day, a mysterious but cleverly named label, #tidalforall, released *The Life of Pablo* "bootleg" on clear vinyl with a limited-edition pressing of only 1,000 copies.

Some of the most exciting aspects of Record Store Day are the events that coincide with the official releases. Since the inception of Record Store Day, artists have supported the event by making appearances or even performing at their local stores. Artists of all caliber head out and support their local record stores during this event. You never know who may make a surprise visit. Notable appearances include The Smashing Pumpkins at Space 15 Twenty during the 2010 Record Store Day. In 2015, Foo Fighters made a surprise appearance at a tiny record shop, the Record Connection in Niles, Ohio. To kick off Record Store Day 2016, the official ambassadors of the event, Metallica, performed live at Rasputin Music in Berkeley, California. Other artists that have made an appearance or performed at local record shops on Record Store Day include Deftones, Beastie Boys, Chuck D, The Beach Boys, Jerry Lee Lewis, Mastodon, Slash, Sick Puppies, Alice in Chains, and more.

Record Store Day event listings and official releases are made available approximately a month before the event. Be sure to determine exactly what titles you are in search of, even prepare a written list beforehand. Do not be afraid to speak to your local record shop(s) to get an idea of what they may be offering. They might not know everything they will receive until a day or two before Record Store Day, but they might know a few things ahead of time. Team up with a friend and head out to different shops to find all the titles on your list.

CHAPTER 11

Vinyl and the Internet

*a*lthough I have already referenced several ways to use the Internet for record collecting, I haven't even begun to scratch the surface. The Internet allows you to research and locate releases that are hard to find. You can use it to find record shops and used record sellers, or even shop directly online in the comfort of your own home. The Internet allows you to connect with similar collectors, whether they are local or on the other side of the planet, making collecting a rewarding social experience.

This chapter highlights a variety of websites and apps that will help you connect with others within the vinyl-collecting community, ease your record-shopping experience, and provides a wealth of resources to help you add to your record collection.

214 Exactly How Did the Internet Fuel the Vinyl Revival?

Although there is no debate that the number of vinyl collectors has spiked since 2006, a sizable number of people have been collecting vinyl before that. Gen-Xers never stopped purchasing vinyl, and a considerable amount of Gen-Y kids took an interest in their parents' hobby of collecting vinyl and began collecting themselves. I have come across quite a few people in their early thirties that have collected vinyl since their teen years. Despite media reports tagging the thirty-something hipster as a trendy follower, vinyl collecting is not new to *all* of them.

If people were collecting vinyl all along, what sparked the revival? In a word: the Internet. The Internet afforded record collectors the ability to connect, share their love with others, and to find records. The vinyl revival was first noticed in 2007 when vinyl record sales in the United States alone climbed to just under 1 million and continued to increase every year following that.

When you examine the total number of vinyl sales, that figure only represents a fraction of the actual vinyl sales. A sizable portion of that number, specifically in North America, is provided through a data-measuring system called Sound-Scan. Neilsen created SoundScan to specifically track the sales of music and movies at major retailers using a product's barcode. A lot of small-scale record retailers, however, do not report their sales to SoundScan. Additionally, artist websites, band merch at concerts, independent online retailers, and other indie retailers often do not report their sales to SoundScan. With a significant amount of record sales happening at the level of independent retail shops, there is definitely a fraction of sales that are not being represented within the SoundScan sales numbers.

LONGEST SONG TITLE

The longest song title belongs to the English electronic/experimental group Test Dept. with their fifty-three-word-long track "Long Live British Democracy Which Flourishes and Is Constantly Perfected Under the Immaculate Guidance of the Great, Honourable, Generous and Correct Margaret Hilda Thatcher. She Is the Blue Sky in the Hearts of All Nations. Our People Pay Homage and Bow in Deep Respect and Gratitude to Her. The Milk of Human Kindness."

In addition, only *new* records are being measured through these sales reports. Particularly through the eighties, nineties, and early millennium, very few new titles were being pressed on vinyl, forcing record collectors to purchase only used records. Used records still represent an enormous portion of collectors' records, with some fanatics exclusively purchasing only used records.

Despite the inability to accurately track actual vinyl record sales for the last few decades, 2007 can be pinpointed as a turning point for the increase of vinyl record sales. The odd thing about this was that it was a terrible time for the music industry, with many music retailers going out of business, CD sales declining, and digital sales not taking off as much as expected. Music sales overall were dwindling immensely due to a combination of music piracy and hard economic times as we entered an economic recession.

This economic climate forced artists and labels to work harder and to become further engaged with their fans. By 2007, numerous social networking sites such as Facebook,

MySpace, Twitter, and reddit allowed not only vinyl collectors to come together and connect, but they allowed artists and labels to actually recognize this society of vinyl collectors and begin to fulfill their demand for vinyl. Some music-based websites, such as Insound, SoundStage Direct, and my company, SRCVinyl, were able to fulfill the demand for vinyl, whereas large retail chains were not as easily able to do so. Those who operated an online music store during 2007 were aware of the presence of a vinyl revolution and were more tuned in to connecting with people online than a considerable amount of brick-and-mortar retailers were. It was an exciting time for those involved in the vinyl industry as both sales and the amount of vinyl fans grew. Vinyl collectors have always existed, but the Internet enabled this group to be visible and encouraged others to explore the possibility of collecting vinyl.

Online Communities

Online networks and communities of vinyl collectors have existed for decades. Specific online communities were created precisely for vinyl devotees, and groups on popular social networking sites such as Facebook and reddit sprung up.

Etiquette

Before I share my treasured vinyl community resources, let's discuss necessary etiquette, saving you face if you're new to these communities. Here are some tips:

- First and foremost, when you join a vinyl community, be sure to review and read the guidelines before jump-

ing in and asking questions or starting a conversation.
A large number of message boards (and other social
networking groups) have particular rules or guidelines
about what you can and can't post. Be sure to review
the rules before posting your first topic.

- Secondly, be sure to search the forum to see if your
question has already been posted before posting
yourself. Forum members frown upon duplicate
posts—especially ones created by forum newbies. If
you can avoid making your first post on a forum the
start of a thread and instead comment on other topics
already there, you are more likely to receive positive
responses from the community.

- Ease your way into the community and learn a bit about
it before jumping in headfirst. Read popular question
threads, check out frequent posters' profiles, and so
on.

reddit

For vinyl collectors of all sorts

The social networking service reddit currently has a vinyl
collector's community with over 94,000 members (www
.reddit.com/r/vinyl). The r/vinyl subreddit allows you to
engage with other collectors and discuss record-buying
subjects including specific releases, creating a turntable
setup, sharing info about records a collector has found, and
just about anything pertaining to vinyl. In addition to this
main vinyl section, reddit has a variety of other vinyl-related
subreddits, including ones for audiophiles, record deals,
hip-hop, vintage, a section for vinyl DJs, and more.

Vinyl Collective

For millennials and Gen-Yers

Suburban Home Records, a record label based out of Denver, Colorado, launched Vinyl Collective (www .vinylcollective.com) in 2006 as a way to release vinyl. At the time of its inception, Vinyl Collective was both an online store for Suburban Home's vinyl releases and a web-based forum for vinyl collectors. During the years Suburban Home owned and ran Vinyl Collective, vinyl sales started taking off and Vinyl Collective played a part in this by reissuing several titles on vinyl.

The forum immediately grew into a collective of vinyl aficionados who were not only sharing their passion for collecting but used this forum to communicate to the Suburban Home staff what releases they wanted on vinyl. Suburban Home would compile this information and work with record labels to release these titles. Vinyl Collective acted as a record label between 2007 and 2011, releasing titles from artists such as Every Time I Die, Drag the River, Joey Cape, Avail, Portugal, The Man, Limbeck, and more.

In January 2011, when Suburban Home discontinued the Vinyl Collective store, my company acquired Vinyl Collective and relaunched the website as a vinyl collector's community and news site (without the store). Currently the Vinyl Collective forum has over 20,000 members and is broken down into five forum boards:

- **Vinyl Collective Message Board:** A general section where you can discuss just about anything pertaining to vinyl records and record releases.
- **Sales/Trades/Wants:** This section is a free way to list records you wish to sell, trade, or are seeking to acquire. With a community of 20,000 vinyl fanatics,

this is an extensive tool for selling and trading records without paying a middleman. When you sell or trade with another user, you are able to rate your experience, forcing users to build a reputation within the selling and trading community. The forum moderators assist monitor for any potential issues and negative feedback provided about a sale or trade, in turn removing misleading or fraudulent sellers and traders from the community.

- **Turntables & Other Audio Equipment:** This is a resource to connect with other members to discuss or seek assistance with your turntable and equipment-related questions. This is an excellent place to explore while you are researching and setting up your new turntable.
- **Everything Else Message Board:** Vinyl Collective has been around for ten years, allowing veteran users to build relationships with each other. This area is a general area to discuss just about anything not related to vinyl such as sports, TV shows, movies, and so on. Each year the Vinyl Collective community also hosts a Secret Santa among members. This is an exclusive annual event that the community members anticipate each year.
- **Cassette Collective:** Due to the amount of interest in cassettes among the vinyl community, a small section dedicated to cassette releases was established.

The musical preferences of the Vinyl Collective community are diverse and span various eras and genres; however, the content skews toward newer titles released from the 1990s to the present, across several genres.

Steve Hoffman Music Forums

For Gen-Xers and baby boomers

The Steve Hoffman Music Forums (http://forums.steve hoffman.tv) were launched in 2001 by audio engineer Steve Hoffman and have grown to an impressively large community of over 55,000 members. With a colossal amount of posts compiled over sixteen years, the Steve Hoffman forums are an exceptional resource of information not found elsewhere. Although the forums are not limited to vinyl and can regularly contain discussions about alternative audio such as SACDs, CDs, and other formats, the majority of the posts pertain to vinyl releases and hardware.

- **Music Corner:** This is the first section on the Discussions part of the forums and is where users can post anything related to music, but with the bulk of content related to discussing vinyl releases.
- **Audio Hardware:** This section is dedicated to discussing audio hardware, but has an abundance of information pertaining specifically to turntables, styluses and cartridges, cleaning records, stereo equipment, and other audio hardware. Many of the collectors on the forum are expert collectors and audiophiles and can be helpful in assisting with or offering advice with complicated turntable and audio questions.
- **Marketplace:** The Marketplace part of the forums is divided into five boards: Third Party Sales & Auctions; Marketplace Discussions; Music, Movie, and Hardware Store Guide; Coupons, Discounts, and Sales; and eBay Watch. This entire section allows users to sell or promote the sale of their records and other audio components.

Although posts are diverse, most of the content appeals to audiophiles and collectors of classic rock, rock, jazz, and other genres appealing to Gen-Xers and baby boomers.

Soul Strut

For DJs and collectors of funk, hip-hop, jazz, and rock

The Soul Strut website (www.soulstrut.com) rightfully boasts the slogan "Since Pretty Much the Dawn of the Internets . . ." as they are a community frequented by vinyl collectors, artists, and DJs since 1999. Genres discussed on the Soul Strut Community threads include 1970s funk, hip-hop, jazz, and rock. The Community offers a general vinyl discussion thread, a want and trade section, a section for discussing DJing, and more.

78rpm Collectors' Community

For collectors of the 78-rpm format

The 78rpm Collectors' Community (www.78rpmcommunity .com) is a social networking website and resource for 78-rpm collectors. The site was launched in 2010 and there is currently over 6,000 members worldwide. It is a no-brainer to check out and join this forum if you intend on collecting 78-rpm records; however, I highly suggest anyone interested in the history of vinyl check it out, especially their Documents section. The History page features a unique collection of record catalogs spanning several eras. The website also has a tremendous photo gallery section featuring multiple 78-rpm albums along with several articles specific to collecting 78s. The forum provides an opportunity to bond with others over different types of music and artists from the 78-rpm era, and it offers the chance to share knowledge pertaining to restoring albums, styluses, phonographs, and needles specific to the 78-rpm format.

Vinyl Engine

Resource for vinyl-related audio hardware
The Vinyl Engine forum (www.vinylengine.com) is a community of over 30,000 members with a focus on discussing audio hardware. Although a board exists for members to converse about music and music releases, the majority of the boards are focused on audio hardware. There are boards for discussing turntables and tone arms, cartridges and preamps, amplifiers and speakers, digital audio, and vinyl ripping. The forum also includes a classifieds area where you can buy and sell both equipment and vinyl records. Lastly, a section is dedicated to specific manufacturers, including various ones I have mentioned in this book such as Marantz, Music Hall, Pro-Ject, Rega, Technics, Thorens, VPI, and more. The Vinyl Engine forum is a tremendous tool for both expanding your vinyl hardware knowledge and to seek reliable assistance with hardware questions.

Facebook Groups

Facebook offers a large number of groups for vinyl collectors. Unlike other vinyl-collecting communities, the majority of the Facebook groups I have come across are specific to a type or the location of a record collector.

It is exciting to be a part of these groups because often this is where you find out about local events such as local record shows in addition to making friends with people in your area who share the same passion for collecting vinyl that you do. On a few occasions I have seen random customers, particularly on Record Store Day, walk up to other random customers they have never met and say something along the lines of, "I recognize you from the Facebook community" and then spend some time hanging out.

How to find Facebook groups in your area:

1. Log onto your Facebook account and type "vinyl records" into the search bar and hit Enter.
2. Select "Group" at the top to assure you are filtering the results to only show groups.
3. Explore the available groups to see if any are appealing to you and close to your region. When I search, the first groups that appear in my search are the ones closest to my region or ones that my friends follow.
4. If the results you receive are not close to your location, try narrowing down your search. First start with your state, for example, "vinyl records New York." Then try something regional such as "vinyl records western New York." If you live in a large city, try searching by neighborhood, such as "vinyl records Park Slope."
5. Be sure each time you search you are selecting to view "Groups"; otherwise, you will pull up a variety of results in addition to Facebook groups.
6. Once you find a group you wish to be a part of, hit the "Join Group" button. Often a group will say it is "Closed." This just means you are required to become a member or be an approved member of that group to view the content. It may require a few days for the moderator of that forum to accept your

request so you may not instantly become a part of the group upon joining.

If you are a collector of a certain genre, such as metal, or a specific type of vinyl, such as 78-rpm albums, try searching Facebook groups using the steps just outlined to find networks that are specific to your interest. Here are a few of my favorite interest-specific Facebook groups:

Chasing the Vinyl Dragon—Collecting Punk Rock Records
Over 9,000 punk-record-collecting members
www.facebook.com/groups/chasingthevinyldragon/

Metal Records with Roger
Over 2,500 metal-collecting members
www.facebook.com/groups/MetalRecordsWithRoger/

80s Hard Rock/Metal Vinyl Collectors
Over 17,000 hard rock and metal members
www.facebook.com/groups/2425072197/

Vinyl/LP Collectors & Trading Group
Over 18,000 members and an excellent group of collectors to trade vinyl with
www.facebook.com/groups/193037070760134/

Vinyl Record Collectors Club
General vinyl-collecting group with over 12,000 members
www.facebook.com/groups/5085864661/?ref=br_rs

The 45s Club—Record Collectors Group
Over 1,000 45-rpm record collectors
www.facebook.com/groups/the45sclub/

Hot Jazz Records
Over 4,000 jazz collectors focused on releases between 1917 and 1931
www.facebook.com/groups/150585181695083/

ReggaeRecords 4 Sale/Trade
A group used by over 5,000 members strictly for selling or trading reggae vinyl
www.facebook.com/groups/228842060490192/

Vinyl LP Advertising
A group of over 3,000 created specifically for the purpose of advertising records for sale within any genre
www.facebook.com/groups/528399867263870/

Vinyl Records Forever
A group of 12,000 members that post vinyl record images
www.facebook.com/groups/414372585320619/

Crate Diggers Union (CDU)
This group has existed since 2007, originally as a group on MySpace. It is a general group of over 4,000 members that appeals to collectors of all sorts.
www.facebook.com/groups/thecratediggersunion

Similar to joining a forum, be sure to review the guidelines of a group and follow their rules for posting.

Vinyl Media and News Online

One of the challenges of collecting vinyl is keeping up with the new releases and reissues. Following is a list of the best websites and ways to be sure you do not miss out on records

226 you may be interested in. Several of the essential music-centric websites, such as Billboard, the Huffington Post, Rolling Stone, and NME, report on vinyl news. And there are also a variety of vinyl-specific websites that are dedicated to exclusively reporting on vinyl releases in detail. These websites are typically created and staffed by writers who are passionate about the vinyl format, so you'll find quality content focused on all things vinyl.

BRAND NEW VINYL

For years, fans of the rock band Brand New clamored for their titles on vinyl particularly *Deja Entendu*, but rarely were the albums ever made available on vinyl. When this album was finally made available on vinyl, preorders were announced on the band's social networks and an assortment of online stores that notified their customers by newsletters. Customers went crazy and stores sold thousands of copies within minutes. People who managed to secure a copy of the initial pressing of this release did so because they signed up on the band's social sites or connected to individual online stores through their newsletters and social websites.

Newsletters and Social Media

Here is a little professional vinyl fanatic secret: The number one way to keep up to date on records from artists you are interested in is to sign up for their e-mail newsletter or follow them on social media. Newsletters are simply e-mails that artists frequently send out to communicate with their fans about tours, new releases, or reissues. In order to sign up for a newsletter, you will need to visit the band's website and find out if they have one available. Often records are announced through the band's website, and some bands offer exclusive vinyl editions available only through them. Follow your favorite artists on social sites and newsletters because if they have a new record or a reissue coming out, they will likely be the first to announce it.

Vinyl Collective

Although Vinyl Collective (www.vinylcollective.com) is primarily a message board, the website also contains news for newly announced vinyl releases and reissues on its main page. Additionally, the forum has news surrounding upcoming releases, often posted frequently within minutes of them being announced, so it's a great place to find out about current vinyl announcements.

SlyVinyl

SlyVinyl (www.slyvinyl.com) is a source for vinyl news but does offer an assortment of other articles, including on equipment, cassettes, and general music posts. Although the amount of news they post is comprehensive, my favorite element of SlyVinyl is their weekly e-mail blast, which features a list of extremely limited and rare records announced that week. SlyVinyl are thorough in their hunt for record news and often talk about titles few others are reporting on.

Modern Vinyl

Staffed by a group of vinyl enthusiasts, the Modern Vinyl website (www.modern-vinyl.com) shares news about upcoming vinyl releases and reissues. They also offer reviews on a variety of titles where they analyze the sound quality, packaging, and any other add-ons included with the release. In addition to frequently checking out the Modern Vinyl website, I suggest following them on Twitter to catch their up-to-date vinyl-release news: https://twitter.com/Modernvinyl.

The Vinyl Factory

The Vinyl Factory (www.thevinylfactory.com) is not just a media site for vinyl collectors; it's a record label, record-pressing plant, and music magazine (*FACT*). The Vinyl Factory website is a great source for vinyl-release news and other vinyl articles covering equipment, record storage, record fairs, and a variety of other topics.

Fun Sites to Visit

Sometimes you don't need any news—you just want to read some fun content about vinyl. Here are two interesting spots to check out.

My Husband's Stupid Record Collection

A little off the beaten path here, but this is one of my favorite vinyl record blogs (http://alltherecords.tumblr.com/). This site is written by a lady named Sarah, who listens to and reviews her husband Alex's record collection of more than approximately 1,500 records, in alphabetical order, one per day. Her husband has a varied and diverse, nongenre-specific collection. Another amusing aspect to her blog are her interpretations and stories she tells about her husband

and his collection. This is a refreshing and a comedic reminder of how the outside world views the weird things we record collectors do.

Dust & Grooves

This is a website dedicated to showcasing vinyl record collectors and their collections. Dust & Grooves (www .dustandgrooves.com) does this by photographing and profiling record collectors and their record rooms. The site is founded and maintained by photographer Eilon Paz, who began making use of his free time by finding and photographing record collections that he believed were larger and weirder than his own. As the project grew, he traveled the world, including North America, Australia, Cuba, Argentina, Ghana, and other regions in search of collectors to document. You can also check out the *Dust & Grooves* book, which profiles over 130 collectors. Both the website and the book feature interviews with collectors and profiles on their collections from all around the world.

Resourceful Websites

Following is a diverse selection of websites that are extremely helpful for collectors. These are the sites that you will rely on to help you build your collection and to find information about releases and audio equipment.

Discogs

I have mentioned Discogs (www.discogs.com) numerous times throughout this book because it is an authoritative and powerful all-in-one tool. Discogs was launched in 2000 as a comprehensive database of user-generated information on electronic music releases. However, Discogs rapidly became the ultimate database for music spanning across every genre. In early 2016, Discogs had a catalog of over 7 million releases by over 4.5 million artists. A little music industry secret to just illustrate how informative Discogs is: I have been in several situations with major-label record executives where we were discussing a release and needed to confirm if their label was the copyright owner of the album. Instead of checking their internal database they almost always consulted the Discogs database. Here are the tools Discogs provides record collectors:

MOST EXPENSIVE RECORDS SOLD ON DISCOGS (AS OF MARCH 2016)

Here are the some of the most expensive records ever sold on Discogs:

- David Bowie *David Bowie* LP ($6,826)
- Leaf Hound *Growers of Mushroom* ($4,329)
- Mammut *Mammut* ($4,010)
- The 4 Levels of Existence *The 4 Levels of Existence* ($2,275)
- Soul Vendors *Happy Ogan* ($2,135)

DISCOGS DATABASE

Their database is extensive, and I have yet to come across a release that I could not find on the Discogs database, and

I have performed a few thousand title searches. Once you find a specific release, the accompanying information typically includes:

- Artist
- Title
- Record label
- Country of release
- Date released
- Genre
- Style
- Track list
- Exact version (details such as record color, specific artwork, markings on the matrix, and any other notes that make that specific release identifiable)
- Other versions
- Sales history (provided as a minimum, median, and maximum amount it has sold for on Discogs)
- Available copies for sale within the Marketplace

DISCOGS COLLECTION

Collectors can easily create a profile and then build a collection by finding the releases they own within the database and adding them to their collection or a want list. The want list allows you to generate a wish list of titles that you do not own but might want to add to your collection. My favorite component about the want list is that you can view other collectors that have your want list items for sale within the Discogs Marketplace, making it extremely easy to acquire the records you desire.

Once you build a collection, you are provided with a direct link to your collection that you can share with others. When you mingle with cyber vinyl-collecting buddies, it is typical to provide them with your Discogs collection link so that you can view each other's collection and possibly trade records. You can check out my collection on Discogs here: www.discogs.com/user/shopradiocast.

DISCOGS MARKETPLACE

Users of Discogs can list music items for sale within the Marketplace and purchase items from other users. When an item is listed for sale, the seller must list the condition of the album using the Goldmine Grading Guide and can also include additional notes on the condition of the record.

Purchases are not regulated directly by Discogs, but payments are processed through PayPal, which provides the buyer with a degree of protection. When you pay a seller for a purchase, request that the seller sends you an invoice through Discogs and not a direct PayPal request e-mail. You will know the difference because the e-mail you receive requesting payment comes from Discogs and not PayPal. This way you can assure that your payment to this seller documents exactly what you ordered.

Lastly, buyers are able to rate sellers and leave comments. Before buying records from a seller you are able to review the seller's ratings and any comments other buyers have left for the seller. The vast majority of the negative comments I encounter on Discogs are in relation to the condition of the record. If you are ever in doubt about a record, do not hesitate to message the user (using the Discogs messaging system) to ask questions about a certain product prior to purchasing.

DISCOGS COMMUNITY

Discogs Community offers forums where you can discuss music with other members and various groups that are specific to types of collections or specific genres, artists, or country. The forums contain sections on a variety of topics in addition to various sections for those who are involved in building the database as well as Marketplace sellers. There are currently over 2,500 different themed groups within the Discogs Community with some groups boasting thousands of members.

DISCOGS APP

The Discogs app is a free app available for Apple devices that allows you to catalog your collection, add to your want list, and view Marketplace pricing for records. The astonishing feature of the app is the ability to enlist your cell phone camera as a barcode scanner allowing you to easily look up releases within the database. Although the Discogs app is currently only available for Apple products, it will soon be available for Android.

eBay

Record collectors seem to have a love/hate relationship with eBay (www.ebay.com), the world's largest online auction house. Even moderate vinyl record collectors will purchase at least one record on eBay at some point. eBay is a magnificent resource for locating rare and collectible records, but they are often priced higher than buying at a retailer. I have a different practice for buying records on eBay. My favorite finds on eBay are through acquiring "lots" of records. When you buy a lot, you buy a designated amount of records, such as twenty-five, fifty, or (if you are crazy like me) even hundreds at one time. You have absolutely no clue what you are buying. You may only be offered limited information on the condition they are in, and on occasion the seller may ask you questions to help curate records you may be interested in. These records are almost always cheaper. I usually pay at most $1 or less per record.

Tips for Buying Records on eBay

- **Know where the seller is located.** If you are buying from a seller outside your country, you may be responsible for shipping and customs fees in addition to the cost of the item.
- **Review the seller's rating.** Consider the amount of ratings they have, not just the quality of their ratings. The more ratings a seller has, the more sales they have completed.
- **When in doubt about anything, whether it be the condition of the record or exact pressing, ask the seller!** Do not be afraid to ask for additional pictures or ask specific questions before making a purchase.
- **Understand the difference between Auction and Buy It Now sales.** When you discover a product with a Buy It Now price, that is the set price for that item. For items that are listed as auctions, you are submitting a competing bid on that item and may be obliged to increase your bid if there is competition.

In addition to buying on eBay, the website can be used as a way to sell extra and duplicate records that you have lying around. Selling on eBay is a fairly simple task but does require you to establish a PayPal account. If you intend on flipping records on eBay, here is a quick checklist to get you started: http://pages.ebay.com/sellerinformation/selling-basics/seller-checklist.html and a thorough guide on how to operate the site as a seller: http://pages.EBay.ca/help/sell/selling-basics.html.

Popsike

The Popsike website (www.popsike.com) is an excellent tool to use along with buying and selling on eBay or buying vinyl just about anywhere. It was created as a tool to easily confirm the value of a vinyl record. Popsike keeps an archive of past auctions, primarily from eBay, and allows you to find the details of these auctions by searching on a title. The true value of a record is based on what people are willing to pay for it, so why not rely on a factual sales history to determine that? Popsike is a free service, but there is a limit on the amount of searches you can complete each day. This number fluctuates based on server load on that day. (I performed a hefty amount of searches before I ran into this issue.)

Popsike also has an app (only available for Apple devices with an Android version coming soon).

VinylHub

VinylHub (www.vinylhub.com) is an extensive, user-generated database for record shops and record events that is owned by Discogs. If you are already a Discogs member, you are not required to sign up to VinylHub. Instead, you just log in with your Discogs account information. On the VinylHub website, you can search for both record shops and events within your area or a location you plan on visiting. To find a store or event, you simply enter your address, a zip code, and a city or province into their search bar. Once you choose a location, complete details for a store or events near you are shown. Each store's profile includes hours, location, contact information, and pictures of that store.

VinylHunt

Similarly to VinylHub, VinylHunt (www.vinylhunt.com) is a website record collectors can utilize to locate record shops near a location they choose. You can enter in your zip or postal code, a city, or a record shop name and a map will pop up showing the record stores located in that area.

Meetup

Meetup (www.meetup.com) is the world's largest network of local groups who share a specific and similar interest. To use this website, you can either browse all the Meetups within a certain distance of your location, or you can enter a type of Meetup within their search bar. For record collectors, typing in "vinyl" should do the trick. Next, include a location and the number of miles within a designated location you are willing to travel, and you should find all the Meetups related to your search in your area.

Record Collectors Guild

The Record Collectors Guild (www.recordcollectorsguild.org) has been online since the early 1990s, making it one of the best sources for appraising and learning about a variety of records and pressings. The website provides a variety of informative articles for record collectors of all types in addition to a thorough guide on how to grade and appraise your records. Quite a few of the articles are unique and offer informative content not found elsewhere.

Vinyl Engine

The Vinyl Engine website (www.vinylengine.com) offers an archive of owner manuals, service manuals, schematics, and brochures for modern and vintage turntables that anyone can access free of charge. Additionally, the website includes reviews of equipment and a Tools section, which has a wide range of articles to assist with turntable setup, how-to guides, and do-it-yourself options.

Phone and Tablet Apps

I have already mentioned the Discogs and Popsike apps, but there are several other apps available that are excellent tools for the record collector. Having an app allows you to stay connected to your newly acquired vinyl while away from the desktop! Here are the apps that are worth downloading, with a lion's share of them free or available for a few dollars.

My Vinyl for Jukebox Owners

Free for Apple
Created for jukebox owners, it allows you to keep track of your record inventory and print jukebox title strips right from your iPhone or iPad.

OnVinyl

Free on Google Play; iOS app coming soon
The OnVinyl app allows record collectors to catalog their collection similar to the Discogs app. Additionally, this app

can be used to note when you loan a record to a friend and to locate record stores. One feature that makes this app unique is its ability to search for details of an album within its database by scanning the cover art with your camera's phone.

The Vinyl District

Free for Android/Apple

This app helps you locate and find out information for brick-and-mortar retail stores throughout thirty-seven countries around the world. In addition to finding record shops, you can check in at the store, provide reviews, and read other users' reviews of specific shops.

Turntabulator

$1.99 Apple

This app allows you to ensure your turntable is playing at the exact speed of 33⅓ or 45 rpm. Simply open the app on your phone, place it on your turntable platter, and start the platter spinning. The app will measure the speed your turntable is spinning within .01 of an rpm. If you ever feel your turntable is spinning at an incorrect speed, this is a quick way to troubleshoot and identify if this the issue.

Vinyl Records Grader EZ

$0.99 Apple

If you are planning to sell your records, this app can help you decide how to grade and appraise your records. The app has you check off details that apply to the condition of your record. Once you complete checking off all the questions regarding the condition, the app provides you a grading for the record's condition, cover condition, and overall value of the record.

VinylWall

Free, Apple and Google Play
Similar to Discogs and OnVinyl, this app allows you to catalog your collection. You can tag record stores where you purchased your albums, follow friends who also collect vinyl, and make new friends who share your passion for collecting vinyl. One feature that sets VinylWall apart is its VinylWall Badges, which are awarded for accomplishing individual record-collecting achievements.

YouTube

Whether you are just beginning your journey as a newbie vinyl collector or you are looking to expand your knowledge, there are millions of videos available on YouTube that can both entertain and educate.

YouTube has a large selection of how-to videos that clearly illustrate step-by-step directions for setting up turntables or cleaning records. If you are considering a certain product, definitely search YouTube to find any potential reviews because you will likely find one in its extensive catalog.

You can also spend hours checking out other collectors who have videotaped their collections. And there are countless reviews of albums for all genres. This is also an extensive resource for learning about those records that are hard to

240   find. Lastly, check out the in-store live performances taped at record shops that are available online. YouTube offers up hours of both educational and entertaining content, making it a valuable resource for collectors.

Glossary of Vinyl Collecting Terms and Acronyms

There are a lot of terms that vinyl collectors use when discussing records and listing records for sale. In addition to slang unique to record collectors, there are quite a few acronyms associated with the buying and selling of records. These acronyms were created to illustrate to both buyers and sellers an accurate description of a record's condition. Following are terms used by vinyl collectors and acronyms you will frequently come across.

#'d
Often used on eBay to reference that the album is numbered.

%CT
Percentage cover torn. When buying or selling a record, this is an acronym the seller uses to tell you about a ripped cover and what percentage the cover is torn.

%LT
Percentage a label is torn.

acetate
A one-off disc made at the lacquer stage, used similarly to a test pressing to verify how a record sounds. It is usually cut by hand in a mastering studio.

alternate take
An alternate recording of a song.

audiophile pressing
Although there are no exact standards to qualify a record as audiophile, this term should mean that the album was pressed using high-quality masters and methods.

BB hole
A small hole on the record jacket that indicates the record is nonreturnable or a promotional item that is not meant for resale.

BL
Stands for blistering, meaning the vinyl has bubbled.

BOC
Bend on cover.

boot
Shortened version of *bootleg.*

bootleg
A release that is unofficially released. Bootleg records can consist of either an illegally duplicated album or an illegally recorded live performance that is sold and circulated on vinyl.

box set
A collection of multiple records within one box or packaging.

BSS
Bottom seam split.

B/W
This is an acronym typically used with a two-sided single 7-inch meaning "backed with." Since 7-inch singles are commonly not titled like albums, they are usually titled with "Song Title A" B/W "Song Title B."

B&W
Black and white.

budget issue
A pressing that was created to be sold below full price.

cat. no.
Catalog number.

CC
This stands for cut corner. Similar to a BB hole, the corner of an album sleeve is cut to indicate a promotional record not intended for resale or cutout record that cannot be returned.

compact 33
A 7-inch single record that was cut at 33⅓ rpm instead of 45 rpm.

crate digging
Going to a record store to look for old records.

cue burn/cue scratching
When a DJ plays a record he places the needle down approximately where the song should begin, then moves the record back and forth while it's on the table to cue the song. This back-and-forth motion rubs and damages the record, creating an identifiable static-sounding noise.

cut out
Same as CC.

CW
Corner wear.

dead wax
The area at the end of the record between the end of the grooves and the center matrix. Also referred to as *lead-out groove*, *end grooves*, or *matrix area*.

deck
Turntable.

deleted
A release that is no longer commercially available.

demo
A demonstration record that is not commercially available.

DHL
Drill hole through label.

die-cut sleeve
A sleeve with a hole in the center.

display card/display flat
A promotional display picture or title card used to promote a release. Typically, a shop owner would use one to display inside the record shop.

DJ only
A record that is issued for the purpose of DJ use only.

DL
Dirty label.

DNAP
Does not affect play.

double groove
A vinyl record that has more than one groove on the side. This allows for hidden tracks on a disc.

dub plate
See *acetate*.

end grooves
The area at the end of the record that is between the end of the grooves and the center matrix. Also referred to as *lead-out groove, matrix area*, or *dead wax*.

EW
Edge wear.

factory custom pressing
An unofficial record that was pressed at an official pressing plant. Sometimes employees of legitimate pressing plants would, illegally, create personal pressings of records.

FC
Front cover.

flipback cover
A record cover that is held together with flaps that fold to the back of the cover from the front.

flipping records
The act of buying a record, then selling it for a higher price than you paid for it.

foldout sleeve
A sleeve that folds out, sometimes into a poster.

freebie
A record given free of charge.

FS
For sale. An acronym used on vinyl sale forums and marketplaces to indicate an item is for sale. For example, "FS: The Smiths—*The Smiths.*"

FT
For trade.

G/F
An acronym used to indicate the jacket is a gatefold.

HTF
Hard to find.

import
A vinyl record that has been pressed in a country different than it is sold in. For example, a UK pressing available in the United States is referred to as an import and vice versa.

interview disc
A record that features spoken word. It can be a promotional item or include coverage of a press conference.

IS
Inner sleeve.

jukebox center
The large center hole on 7-inch records that is used for playback in jukeboxes.

lead-in groove
The silent area at the beginning of a record.

lead-out groove
The area at the end of the record that is between the end of the grooves and the center matrix. Also referred to as *dead wax, end grooves,* or *matrix area.*

LLP
Little long playing; a 7-inch record that plays at 33⅓ rpm.

locked groove
A groove that is created to intentionally repeat every turn of the record.

LS
Lightly scratched.

lunched
A record in such poor condition that it is unplayable; it looks like someone attempted to eat it for lunch.

LW
Label wear.

marble vinyl
When multiple vinyl colors are mixed together in a marbling effect. No two marbled records are alike!

matrix area
The area at the end of the record that is between the end of the grooves and the center matrix. Also referred to as *lead-out groove, end grooves,* or *dead wax.*

Maxi-single
A term used to indicate an EP.

mispress
Indicates that a record has incorrect tracks or track order.

MO
Mail order.

M/S
This means mono/stereo. In the 1960s, 45s would include the same song with it mono on one side and stereo on the other side.

machine stamped
As opposed to hand inscribing the matrix numbers into the dead wax, some labels preferred to die cut the letters. Die-cut matrix numbers are referred to as machine stamped.

N/R
Nonreturnable.

NAP
Not affect play. This is used when selling a record that has scratches or scuffs that do not affect the way the record sounds.

newbie, noobie
Someone who is new to vinyl collecting.

numbered, No'd
A limited-edition album that is individually numbered.

OIS
Original inner sleeve.

OOP
Out of print. Refers to a record that is out of print and no longer available for purchase in new condition.

original label
The company that first released a certain title.

OS
Outer sleeve.

OST
Original soundtrack.

PO
Pre order, the act of purchasing a record prior to the release date. This is common within the music industry. Many records are put up for purchase weeks, even months before the release date with entire pressings selling out before the actual release date.

PPL
Poorly pasted label.

PS, P/S
Picture sleeve.

push marks
Little circular indentations under the center label of a record, usually found on collectible Sun Records 45s.

R 'n' R
Rock-and-roll.

R-A-B
Rockabilly.

radio spots
Records containing promotional advertisements used at radio stations.

recycled vinyl
When virgin vinyl is pressed into a record and then destroyed. The center label is punched out of the album and the remainder of the vinyl is melted down and reused.

repaired seam
This is when someone has repaired the seam of a record jacket. This can be done by gluing the jacket together or sometimes using tape.

reverse groove
The groove plays in the opposite direction, from the inside to the outside of the record. To play a reverse groove you place the needle at the end of the record and begin playback as you normally would for any other record.

RI
Reissue.

ring wear, RW
A circular discoloration on the record jacket that is caused by improperly storing the LP inside the record jacket. This can also happen with new records that are shrink-wrapped too tightly.

run-out groove
The groove at the end of the record.

RSC
Radio station copy.

RSD
Record Store Day.

seam
The edge of a record jacket.

seam split
When the edge of a record jacket has split or cracked open.

SCR
An acronym used to indicate a scratch on the record.

SCU
An acronym used to indicate a scuff on the record.

SLT/WRP, SLW
An acronym used to indicate a slightly warped record.

SM/SPLIT
An acronym used to indicate a seam split. Can include a percentage to represent what percentage of the seam is split.

SOBC
Sticker on back cover.

SOC
Sticker on cover.

SOL, STOL
Sticker on label.

spine
The thicker edge of a record sleeve where the artist name, album title, and catalog number are printed.

splatter vinyl
A record with assorted colors sprinkled together in a splatter effect.

SPLT/SM, SPS
Indicates a split seam. Can include a percentage to represent what percentage of the seam is split.

SS
Still sealed.

T.P.
Test pressing.

tape/OBC
Tape on back cover.

tape/OC
Tape on cover.

tape/OL
Tape on label.

timing strip
A strip on the cover of promo items that is usually glued to the cover. This is used to show the title and playing time of each song.

TOBC
Tear on back cover.

TOC
Tear on cover.

TOL
Tear on label.

track list
The selection of tracks on a release.

TS
Taped seams.

uncut picture disc
Test pressing of a shaped picture disc that is circular. On occasion, shaped picture discs are not cut during the test-pressing stage and instead are circular, unlike the commercial release, which is shaped. These are very rarely available for sale.

Various Artist, V/A
Release containing tracks from various artists.

vinyl junkie
This is the most dedicated vinyl collector; someone who dedicates most of his or her free time to hunting or playing vinyl.

wax
A slang term used primarily in North America to refer to vinyl.

white label promo, WLP
A promotional record that has a white center label. Typically found on promos, demos, and test pressings.

withdrawn
A record that has been removed from sale by the manufacturer. Despite the record being withdrawn, there are typically some copies that exist in the market making withdrawn records highly desirable to collectors.

WOBC
Writing on back cover.

WOC
Writing on cover.

WOL
Writing on label.

WRP
A warped record.

WSOBC
Water stain on back cover.

WSOC
Water stain on cover.

WSOL
Water stain on label.

WTB
Want to buy.

WTT
Want to trade.

WTS
Want to sell.

WTTF
Want to trade for.

Top Indie Record Stores

Visiting indie stores is a rewarding experience for record collectors. You will likely leave the store not only with a quality find but often with a memorable experience, whether it is making a friend or learning something new. Even if you don't bond with other collectors, a quality indie store will have a vast selection to browse through, and you are likely to come across something exciting.

It is common for record collectors to travel around and visit some of the best record shops in the world. If you ever have the opportunity to visit any of the following stores, you will be rewarded with an authentic record collector's experience and just might score some noteworthy records.

Amoeba Records (California)
With multiple locations throughout California, including Berkeley, San Francisco, and Hollywood, Amoeba is a definite stop when visiting the Golden State. The Amoeba stores are fairly large in size compared to other independent record stores. Although they sell CDs, DVDs, laser discs, VHS, and other media types, they have a large selection of both new and preowned vinyl. The Hollywood location has two floors with the first floor all music.

Amoeba Records frequently enlists top-notch artists to perform live instore, with past acts including artists such as Deftones, Shooter Jennings, Bob Mould, Neko Case, The Black Keys, Norah Jones, Paul McCartney, Elvis Costello, Lana Del Rey, and more. If you are ever in Berkeley, San Francisco, or Hollywood, be sure to stop at Amoeba because you are guaranteed to find something worthy to add to your collection.

Bananas Music (St. Petersburg, Florida)
Vinyl collectors have planned entire vacations around visiting Bananas in St. Petersburg, which has over 3 million records. Not to mention they offer a diverse catalog featuring classical music, blues, new releases, and rare records from all over the world.

Dund Gol Records (Ulaanbaatar, Mongolia)
In 2015, the capital of Mongolia, Ulaanbaatar, got its first record store! This is possibly one of the world's most isolated record shops, but it started off with a collection of more than 3,000 records! Before the opening of Dund Gol, the people of Mongolia had to travel to Beijing, which is 600 miles away, in order to collect vinyl.

Forever Young Records (Texas)
Forever Young Records, in Grand Prairie, Texas, is a ridiculously large record shop carrying approximately 25,000 new and used records in addition to cassettes, CDs, posters, reel tapes, and other music memorabilia. If you

follow Forever Young on Facebook, you'll see that each week they post a variety of stock updates on both new and secondhand vinyl records.

Generation Records (New York, New York)
If you are on the hunt for older and hard-to-find metal, punk, ska, and reggae records, Generation in New York City is a bucket-list must. At first, Generation Records may seem like a tiny shop, but when you head downstairs you will find an expansive selection of punk, rock, and jazz records in addition to band apparel.

George's Song Shop (Johnstown, Pennsylvania)
The oldest record store in the United States, this store was founded in 1932 by Bernie George, who ran it until his son, John George, took over in 1962. If you don't make it out to visit this shop, be sure to check out their website, which includes some historic photos of America's oldest record shop: www.georgessongshop.com.

Grimey's (Nashville, Tennessee)
Nashville is a music town, and Grimey's pays homage to that with not only an extremely well-stocked record shop but with their in-store performances as well. Live performances have included the likes of larger, mainstream artists such as Metallica, Phoenix, and The Black Keys, in addition to several local indie, rock, and country musicians. If visiting Nashville, a visit to Grimey's will definitely reward you with reasonably priced finds and a likelihood of seeing a brilliant artist perform live.

People's Records (Detroit, Michigan)
Although People's Records lost practically everything in a 2008 fire, in true Detroit fashion, the store bounced back growing into one of the best thrift record shops in the United States. People's Records now has two Detroit locations, and both carry only preowned records specializing in soul, funk, blues, and jazz. The store is popular not only with the locals, but its expansive selection attracts DJs from all over the world.

Princeton Record Exchange (Princeton, New Jersey)
Located just an hour outside of New York City, Princeton Record Exchange is a reasonably priced record shop with an expansive selection. The store carries an extremely diverse collection of genres, making this a must-visit for collectors of all sorts.

Redlight Records (Amsterdam, Netherlands)
Housed in the red light district of Amsterdam, Redlight Records is a tiny record shop with a sizable selection. It carries a variety of cheap records and rarities including electronic, house, prog, rock, funk, disco, and jazz.

Rocking Horse Records (Brisbane, Australia)

Celebrating over forty years of being in business, Rocking Horse is one of the earliest, if not the oldest, record store in Australia. Over the years, I have connected with various Australian collectors and have learned how difficult it is to acquire vinyl in Australia due to the lack of music distribution within the country. Despite these difficulties, Rocking Horse carries an extensive and diverse stock of both new and used vinyl and CDs.

Sonic Boom Records (Seattle, Washington)

With a large collection of both new and preowned records spanning genres like rock, electronic, hip-hop, and jazz, Sonic Boom is a top spot for collectors. Sonic Boom is recognized by *Rolling Stone* magazine as one of the best record shops in the United States.

Spillers Records (Cardiff, Wales)

Established in 1894 by Henry Spiller, Spillers Records is recognized as the world's oldest record shop by *Guinness World Records*. It remained in its original location up until it relocated to a nearby location in 2010 and then again to a bright and large space in 2015. Spillers carries a diverse selection of records and has an authentically friendly and service-oriented staff.

Tower Records (Shibuya, Tokyo, Japan)

Tower Records in Japan was left unscathed by the 2006 Tower Records bankruptcy because it became independent from the international chain in 2002. It's not an indie store because Tower Records Japan (TJR) is a chain, but the flagship store in Shibuya, Tokyo, merits a listing here. It is an insanely large store boasting over 53,000 square feet spread across nine floors. The Shibuya Tower Records location has an extensive collection of music, including an entire floor dedicated to classical music.

Waterloo Records (Austin, Texas)

Waterloo opened up in Austin, Texas, in 1982, prior to the launch of the renowned South by Southwest festival and before the Austin music scene really took off. Waterloo Records is known for allowing customers to listen to any record in the store, and customers can return an album for any reason up to ten days after purchase. The selection at Waterloo is especially diverse, and all the albums are displayed together in simple alphabetical order, not broken out by genre, something I really appreciate as it promotes expanding your mind while digging through records because you're not focusing on just a single genre at a time.

The Winnipeg Record & Tape Co. (Winnipeg, Canada)

Although located in one of Canada's smaller cities, the Winnipeg Record & Tape Co. is known for its collection of sealed original pressings. This is a dreamy record store for collectors of soul, funk, disco, and jazz.

Index

Acoustic era, 37
American Graphophone
Company, 18
Analogue Productions, 194–95
Artwork, 47–49, 189–91
Atlantic Records, 201
Audiophile, 112–13

Blood-filled records, 33
Bootleg records, 145, 210

Capitol Records, 200–201
Car stereos, 24–25
Cartridge, replacing, 77–81, 108–9
Catalog numbers, 186
CDs, 113–14, 138, 140–42, 178,
193–97
Cleaning records
dry-cleaning methods, 176–78
methods to avoid, 168, 170,
178–80
record-cleaning machines,
174–76
wet-cleaning methods, 169–74
Collector terminology, 111–20,
241–47
Collector tips, 183–211. See also
Record collections
Columbia Records, 18, 22–23, 25,
48, 143
Cover art, 47–49, 189–91
Craigslist, 73, 129, 134, 159

Dead wax area, 113, 115, 187–88
Digital era, 38
Direct metal mastering (DMM),
115
Discogs, 123–24, 132–33, 230–33
DVDs, 141–42, 144, 178

eBay, 76, 133–34, 233–34
Edison Records, 14–17
Electrical era, 37

Etchings, 32, 116

Facebook, 129, 215–16, 222–25
Fidelity, 13
Filled records, 32–34
Flexi discs, 30–31
Friday Music, 196

Glossary of terms, 241–47
Gramophone, 12
Graphophone, 11

Handling records, 105–6, 148–49

Ice record project, 32
Indie record stores, 137–38,
249–51
Insurance, 162–65
Internet
how-to videos, 239–40
online communities, 216–25
online news, 225–28
online retailers, 140–45
resources on, 213–40
social networking sites, 129,
215–17, 221–26
tablet/phone apps, 237–39

Jacket condition, 122–23
Jacket types, 47–49, 116–17

Kijiji, 73, 129, 134

Laser turntables, 101. See also
Turntables
Laser-etched vinyl, 32
Legacy Recordings, 196–97
Light in the Attic Records, 197–98
Liquid-filled records, 32–33
LP descriptions, 117–18

Magnetic era, 37–38
Mastering, 114–15

Materials, 25–31. *See also* Production process
Matrix area, 115
Matrix markings, 187–89
Mobile Fidelity Sound Lab, 113, 198–99
Mondo Music, 33, 199–200
Monophonic sound, 38–39
MySpace, 216, 225

New records. *See also* Records
  bootleg records, 145
  considerations for, 119–20, 136–37
  finding, 137–45
  online retailers, 140–45
  purchasing, 135–46
New turntables. *See also* Turntables
  budget for, 81–83, 86, 90, 94, 97–98
  considerations for, 81–83
  models, 83–101

Online communities, 216–25
Online news, 225–28
Online retailers, 140–45

Phonautograph, 10
Phone apps, 237–39
Phonographs, 10–11, 14, 37
Pickwick Records, 29–30
Picture discs, 28–30
Plating process, 42. *See also* Production process
Preamp, 63–65
Pressings
  different pressings, 185–91
  filled pressings, 32–34
  first pressings, 191–92
  identifying, 190–91
  original pressings, 191–92
  production process, 32–36, 43–47
  test pressings, 43–44, 208–9
  unusual pressings, 31–34
Prestige Records, 25

Production process
  artwork, 47–49
  jackets, 47–49
  lacquer, 40–42
  overview of, 36
  plating, 42
  pressings, 32–36, 43–47
  record materials, 25–31
  sound playback, 38–40
  sound recordings, 36–38
Promotional records, 206–8. *See also* Records
Purchasing records
  considerations for, 119–21, 136–37
  examining records, 122–25
  finding records, 128–34, 137–45
  grading records, 126–28
  new records, 135–46
  used records, 121–34
Purchasing turntables. *See also* Turntables
  budget for, 74, 77–101
  considerations for, 69–73, 81
  examining turntables, 74–76
  laser turntables, 101
  new turntables, 81–101
  online purchases, 76
  purpose of, 69–71
  recommended models, 77–81
  used turntables, 71–81
  vintage turntables, 71–81

Quadraphonic sound, 40

RCA Victor, 16, 19, 22–23, 27
Receivers, 65–66, 102
Record clubs, 143–44
Record collections
  artwork identifiers, 189–91
  catalog numbers, 186
  choosing records for, 184–85, 209–11
  collector tips, 183–211
  insuring, 162–65
  interesting collections, 228–29
  Internet resources, 213–40

largest collection, 162
matrix markings, 187–89
pressing options, 185–93,
    208–9
promotional records, 206–8
terminology, 111–20, 241–47
test pressings, 208–9
valuable records, 209
vinyl reissues, 193–206
Record frames, 161
Record jackets, 47–49, 116–17,
    122–23
Record labels, 14–19, 194–206
Record shows, 131–32
Record sleeves, 47–49, 118–19,
    152–56
Record storage tips, 147–66
Record Store Day, 32, 34, 209–11,
    223
Record stores, 128, 137–39,
    249–51
Records
    advanced collections, 183–211
    bootleg records, 145, 210
    cleaning, 167–78
    colored records, 27–28
    commercialization of, 12–13
    evolution of, 20
    examining, 122–25
    filled records, 32–34
    grading, 126–28
    handling tips, 105–6, 148–49
    history of, 9–31, 37–38
    insuring, 162–65
    Internet resources, 213–40
    materials for, 25–31
    new records, 119–20, 135–46
    old versus new, 119–20
    online communities for, 216–25
    online news on, 225–28
    parts of, 44–45
    picture discs, 28–30
    pressings, 31–36, 43–47, 185–
        93, 208–9
    production of, 35–49
    promotional records, 206–8
    purchasing new, 135–46

purchasing used, 121–34
reissues, 193–206
repairing, 180–81
RPMs of, 20–25
scratched records, 180–81
speeds of, 20–25
spinning records, 105
storage tips, 147–66
unusual pressings, 31–34
used records, 121–34
valuable records, 209
warped records, 180
websites about, 228–40
weight of, 116
wet records, 105, 168
reddit, 216, 217
Reissues, 193–206
Remastering, 114
Retailers, 137–45
Revolutions per minute (RPMs),
    20–25
Rhino Records, 200–201

Scratched records, 180–81
Social networking sites, 129, 215–
    17, 221–26
Sony Music, 196–97
Sound playback, 38–40
Sound recordings, 36–38
Speakers, 66–68, 102
SRCVinyl, 8, 94, 142–43, 152, 158,
    201–2
Stereophonic sound, 39–40
Storage tips, 147–66
Stylus, cleaning, 107–8
Stylus, replacing, 77–81, 108–9
Subscription services, 143–44
Sundazed Music, 202–3

Tablet apps, 237–39
Third Man Records, 32, 144, 203–6
Time Warner, 201
Tracking force, 104–5
Turntables
    automatic operation, 62–63
    belt-driven turntable, 61
    caring for, 105–9

256

Turntables—*continued*
  cartridge for, 55, 77–81, 108–9
  cleaning, 106–8
  components of, 52–60, 63–68,
    71–75
  direct-drive turntable, 61–62
  dust cover on, 53, 106
  idler-wheel turntable, 63
  laser turntables, 101
  manual operation, 62–63
  new turntables, 81–101
  platter of, 53, 74, 105
  preamp for, 63–65
  purchasing, 66–68
  receiver for, 65–66, 102
  replacing parts, 108–9
  setting up, 71–72, 101–5
  speakers for, 66–68, 102
  stylus for, 54, 77–81, 107–9
  terminology on, 52–63
  tracking force, 104–5
  used turntables, 71–81
  vintage turntables, 71–81
Twitter, 216, 228

Used records. *See also* Records
  considerations for, 119–20
  examining, 122–25
  finding, 128–34
  grading, 126–28
  online resources, 132–34
  purchasing, 121–34
Used turntables. *See also*
  Turntables
  budget for, 74
  considerations for, 69–73
  examining, 74–75
  finding, 73–74, 76
  models, 77–81
  parts for, 77–81

Valuable records, 209
Victor Talking Machine, 19. *See
  also* RCA Victor
Vintage turntables, 71–81. *See
  also* Used turntables
Vinyl records. See Records

Vogue Records, 29
Volta Graphophone Company, 11,
  18
Voyager spacecraft records, 29

Warner Music, 201
Warped records, 180
Waxwork Records, 205–6
Western Electric, 37

X-ray records, 31

YouTube videos, 74, 239–40